MADE FIT FOR GOD IN THAT AFFLICTION

by Robert M. Claytor

"For affliction is a treasure, and scarce any man has enough of it; no man hath affliction enough that is not matured and ripened by it and made fit for God in that affliction."

Meditations from Devotions upon Emergent Occasions # XVII, by John Donne

Bedewrite Press
40 Morris Mill Road
Staunton, Virginia 24401
iona563@cfw.com
1996

Grateful acknowledgment is made for permission to reprint from the following:

Excerpts from *Alcoholics Anonymous*. Copyright © 1939, 1955, 1976 by Alcoholics Anonymous World Services, Inc. Reprinted by permission of Alcoholics Anonymous World Services, Inc. Permission to reprint this material does not mean that A.A. agrees with the views expressed herein. A.A. is a program of recovery from alcoholism <u>only</u> – use of this material in connection with programs and activities which are patterned after A.A., but which address other problems, or in any other non-A.A. context does not imply otherwise.

Excerpt from *Telling Secrets* by Frederick Buechner, copyright © 1991 by Frederick Buechner. Reprinted by permission of the author.

Excerpt from *The Civil War, A Narrative*, Vol. 3, by Shelby Foote, copyright © 1974 by Shelby Foote. Reprinted by permission of the author.

Excerpts from *Memories of God* by Roberta Bondi, copyright © 1995 by Abingdon Press. Reprinted by permission of Abingdon Press.

Excerpt from sermon by the Reverend Ted Loder of the First United Methodist Church of Germantown, Philadelphia, PA. Reprinted by permission of author.

Wicket Gate text reprinted by permission of The Educational Center, Clayton Road, St. Louis, Missouri.

Copies of Made Fit for God In That Affliction may be purchased through Bedewrite Press, 40 Morris Mill Road, Staunton, Virginia 24401. (540) 886-6008

Second Printing 1997

ISBN 0-9653186-0-5

For Marilyn and Mike

Contents

Appendices

Preface

This book is about the spiritual journey to recovery from addiction. It is not a book about religion, although some may misunderstand it as that. Members of Alcoholics Anonymous and Narcotics Anonymous insist their recovery programs are "spiritual but not religious." While such a distinction is clear as a fresh-cleaned windshield to them, it is fuzzy to many others. I wrote this to clear away fuzziness, but also to explain why abstinence without spirituality lacks fecundity and passion. It has no soul. Unless spirituality permeates physical and mental recovery, sobriety will likely wither and die.

This book was written for healers and those desiring to be healed: substance abuse counselors, pastoral counselors, psychiatrists, psychologists, clinical social workers, professional counselors, marriage and family counselors, other clinicians, chaplains, clergy, addicts, alcoholics and their families.

What is written here has come from my experience working in substance abuse treatment since 1972. I have counseled and consulted in state and federal agencies, privately owned treatment centers and my own private practice. I have taught student substance abuse counselors in college classrooms and have been clinical supervisor to others in their agencies.

Although this book is classified as non-fiction, I have used some fictional characters, each a pseudonym, each a composite of hundreds of Leroys, Doras, Freds, Junes, Big Georges, Little Georges, Claires and Mr. Babcocks.

I have had many mentors, especially Mike Claytor, Marilyn Claytor, Charles Durbin, Cecil, Sam C., Con M., Jim Holes, the late Bill Oglesby and the late A. W. Jeffries. I am forever grateful for Fitz Allison, who taught me about Luther's understanding of justification by faith through the Pauline-Greek word *logidzomai,* and for Jack Gessell, who taught me to integrate a theological curriculum. My students have taught me far more than they realize.

Doug Mouk, Simon Jackson, Charles Durbin and Greg Dodge read the manuscript and made helpful suggestions. Art Steele gave me helpful critique for the pharmacological parts of Chapter Three. My editor,

Rebecca Chaitin, corrected, cleaned, polished and shined it. My graphic designer, Brad Robison, put it all together in its final form. Any mistakes remaining are my own.

Most of what I know about alcoholism, addiction and recovery I learned not from the professionals but from: 1. my friends in Alcoholics Anonymous, Al-Anon, and Narcotics Anonymous, 2. my patients, who have struggled, contended and argued with me and their disease.

Some of my patients have made it through the passageways safely to long-term recovery. Others were wounded and broken along the way, but eventually made it through. Many have died en route. Others became permanently disabled by accidents when they were drunk or high. Some are still in the passageways. It is from these "living, human documents"[1] that I have learned the most.

Robert M. Claytor
Staunton, Virignia
September, 1996

Chapter I
The Membrane Mind

Ideally, an addict or alcoholic in full, long-term recovery enjoys a functioning body, a healthy mind, significant relationships and a robust spiritual life. Unfortunately, too many never realize this potential. I believe this is in large part because of professional confusion in treatment programs. I hope to bring clarity to this confusion.

The passageways to recovery are very confusing, at times frightening, often paradoxical, sometimes simple, as well as alternately funny and even boring. Addicts on their way to recovery change their thinking again and again. Their feelings and attitudes keep changing. If they are able, they allow themselves to be grasped and shaken with the realization that they can win only through surrender. If they are able, they resign themselves to their helplessness in the face of the drug. But with that acceptance they discover a new power in their lives, a community power surrounding them in the body of the Twelve Step groups. Among the "we" they can do what "I" could not.

If this spiritual shake-up (what C. G. Jung called "huge emotional displacements and rearrangements")[2] does not occur in them, their recovery will not begin, or if begun, cannot be sustained.

The whole person has become addicted: body, mind and soul. Full recovery requires physical, mental and spiritual healing.

The confusion experienced by addicts and alcoholics in early recovery is matched by a parallel confusion on the part of their healers. We are all a bit mystified with distinctions of mind, body and soul.

The ways we understand body and mind overlap each other. For instance, an ophthalmologist can diagnose a kind of blindness impervious to treatment with glasses, medicine or surgery. Called conversion hysteria, this condition requires psychiatric treatment. The problem is "only" mental, some will say, as if that made the blindness less severe. An illness of the mind has overlapped into the body.

Distinctions between soul and mind are even more murky. In the language of ancient Greece, from which most medical terms are fashioned, *psyche* more often than not meant soul. Most often the Greeks used the word *nous* when they spoke of mind. Yet on occasion they would use *nous* to mean soul and *psyche* to mean mind. Although the ancient Greeks had no such word as "psychiatrist"[3] they would have thought it meant some sort of a priest, a "doctor of the soul".

My point is that from ancient times until today the boundaries between "mind" and "soul" have been murky.

When we say addiction is a physical, mental and spiritual disease, that is also confusing. It has always been confusing and probably will be for a long, long time to come.

* * *

Although they are unaware of it, addicts are in bondage, as if they were in a straitjacket, blindfolded and imprisoned in a modern purgatory. Their impairment is threefold:

A. **Physical addiction** is the straitjacket, but this straitjacket is hidden beneath the skin, a constraint of an addict's idiosyncratic metabolism, receptor sites, DNA code and body chemicals with long names like norepinephrine, dopamine, serotonin and acetaldehyde dehydrogenase. Addiction is physical. The unseen straitjacket reinforces the habit, adapts to it and quietly does its work even while the addict is sleeping.

B. **Mental addiction** is the blindfold. Its wrapping is also hidden beneath the skin, the skin covering the skull. It is a gauze of tricks of the primitive brain, active even while the body enjoys its vacations on beaches of sedation and euphoria. It develops a never-ending succession of strategies for refusing to see the obvious, blaming others, excusing itself and explaining things away. The unconscious part of the addicted mind is on the job twenty-four hours a day.

C. **Spiritual addiction** is the subtle, powerful, invisible purgatory which envelops the alcoholic. The user trusts the drug, believes in it. This belief has reached the level of a profound faith. It "saves" the addict from normal anxiety and everyday frustration . Whatever "saves" one is by definition a savior. The drug has much *worth-ship*. (Long ago in Anglo-Saxon times we contracted "worth-ship" into "worship".) Addicts got what they *thought* they wanted! Sojourners in Dante's *Purgatory* were initially seduced into those realms by getting what they thought they wanted.

A MEMBRANE MIND WITH SEPARATE CHAMBERS

As addiction treatment became a modern specialty, its practitioners readily drew on the expertise of modern medicine, psychology and spirituality. Unfortunately, late in this century the practitioners of these three disciplines have grown metaphorical membranes (in their own heads) to isolate themselves and their thinking from one another. Then physicians, psychotherapists and theologians went into their separate chambers to think, practice, study and train students. You might call it compartmentalized thinking.

ABD (all-but-dissertation) Ph.D. candidates understand this well. Their advisors have constantly told them to narrow their focus until they have a manageable arena of original research. One of my mentors used to joke that he learned more and more about less and less until he knew almost everything about virtually nothing.

Professionals specialize. Physicians treat bodies. Psychiatrists and psychologists treat minds. Ministers are trained in the "cure" of souls. Professionals narrow their focus so they will know what to do. It has to be this way, else the scope of the professions would be beyond anyone's grasp. Unfortunately the membrane walls isolate thinking.

Holistic medicine is the recognition of and a reaction to this membrane mindset, but often the empirical-brained scientist mistrusts the holistic healer, imagining her/him as some wierdo wearing robes and beads, meditating with a crystal.

The membrane mindset is a major problem in substance abuse treatment.

* * *

Physical signs such as body temperature, dilation of eye pupils, blood pressure, urine screens, liver sensitivity to finger poking and blood alcohol levels offer data for empirical measurement. Drugs to ease withdrawal and prevent convulsions can be prescribed by physicians. Antabuse and naltrexone will block receptor sites for a short while.

Psychotherapists bring their interpersonal skills and *the way they were trained to think* into the addiction treatment center. Sometimes they ask the wrong questions. They may ask the relapsed alcoholic *why* he drank, *why* she took that first drink. Alcoholics rarely know why. The question itself betrays a lack of understanding of the spirituality of recovery from addiction. Successfully recovering addicts[4] understand that *if* their spiritual condition is right they will not drink, no matter what, "not even if their ass falls off."

With the exception of a few certified pastoral counselors, some clinical pastoral education supervisors and a handful of sophisticated clergy engaged in the treatment of addiction, the spiritual dimension has mostly been abandoned by the other professionals. There are some happy exceptions. Although neither claims to have a theological education, psychiatrists Gerald May and Scott Peck have made impressive attempts at stretching the membranes. Because of that some of their colleagues consider them suspect, lacking empirical purity.

Naive preachers have clung to the hope that a religious conversion alone would bring permanent recovery from addiction. Except "here and there, once in a while"[5] this does not work either. The secular psychotherapeutic disciplines sometimes trivialize this spiritual conversion approach, yet in so doing they miss a crucial understanding. Rarely does recovery endure without some kind of spiritual awakening.

Spirituality alone rarely brings recovery; neither does counseling or treatment without it.

* * *

As those in recovery from addiction leave their treatment centers and continue their journey in Alcoholics Anonymous, Narcotics Anonymous and Cocaine Anonymous, they must eventually face deeper into the spiritual realms.

They learn and re-learn about addiction, one day at a time, as a threefold illness with a threefold recovery. First, their bodies begin to function better. Next, as the fog of the mind clears, they become less defensive, less defiant and grandiose. Finally, spiritual issues emerge. They begin to concern themselves with the will of God-as-they-understand-Him and the destiny of their lives.

Then one night at an AA meeting they hear an old-timer say, "It's *all* spiritual. The whole program is spiritual." They are puzzled.

It is this puzzle we concern ourselves with in the pages ahead. Yes, recovery is three fold, and yet, it is all spiritual.

If it sounds as if I am contradicting myself, it is because I am. The truth here is paradoxical. As yet there is no reliable cure for addiction. Yet many addicts and alcoholics find a lifelong spiritual method, a one-day-at-a-time way to arrest the disease, much as a diabetic can arrest diabetes.

I suspect it is going to be this way for a long time to come, maybe forever and ever, world without end.

In order to make my case for spirituality as all-encompassing, I must discuss the three dimensions of addiction at length. (This discussion is in

Chapter Three.) Before that I would like to explore the subject of denial. All addicts and alcoholics deny their disease; most of the time their family members deny it too. Even we professionals sometimes have trouble seeing what is right in front of us.

ENDNOTES

1. A term from the early clinical pastoral education movement, probably attributable to Anton Boisen.

2. As quoted in *Alcoholics Anonymous*, Alcoholics Anonymous World Services, Inc. NY, 3rd edition, 1976, page 27.

3. No such term appears in *Liddell and Scott's Greek English Lexicon*, Oxford, 1953.

4. My use of the word "addict" here includes alcoholics: i.e., those addicted to the sedative drug alcohol, also called beverage alcohol. For most purposes in this book the terms are interchangeable.

5. C. G. Jung, as quoted *Alcoholics Anonymous*, loc. cit.

Chapter II
Invincible Ignorance

"If he just made up his mind, I'm sure he could quit. His Uncle Egbert did."

Yes, his uncle did stop drinking whisky completely, but her Fred, well, he can't — or won't — she's really not sure.

There are some, like Egbert, who can stop on their own. E. M. Jellinek called them "beta" alcoholics.[1] I just call them drunks. They could stop, if they would; they just won't. They are irresponsible drinkers, like people who drive too fast and break into line in front of you.

Then there is Fred. He is not a drunk; he's an alcoholic. Jellinek would classify him as a "gamma" alcoholic, the kind most often found in Alcoholics Anonymous. If Fred could stop drinking, he would.

So, Egbert could if he would, and did.

Fred would if he could, but can't.

However!

It's not quite so simple, as you already knew.

You see, Fred, who can't stop, *thinks* he can stop. His wife, June, keeps asking him to stop (thinking he can keep such a promise) and he keeps promising to quit. In fact he told his buddy, Sam, "Hell, I can quit...anytime I want. I just don't want to, although that day may have to come soon."

Beta alcoholics (common drunks) give real alcoholics (gamma alcoholics) a bad name. Betas get religion and quit. Uncle Egbert went to his doctor, who told him to quit because of the ravages to his gastrointestinal tract. He quit.

So June sent Fred to their doctor. Dr. Smith told Fred to quit drinking booze for the sake of his high blood pressure. He told Fred his liver was enlarged and said his pancreas was in trouble.

That evening Fred had two hefty drinks of Scotch. He went to bed early but never really could get to sleep. He worried for several hours. He felt guilty. Then he got angry at that nice old Dr. Smith, even thought of not paying for the visit!

Fred cannot stop, but from behind his blindfold he is unable to see that. He cannot see his straitjacket. He is frustrated and angry with himself for failing again, but he finds it easier to blame someone else than to face his bondage. Such blaming and feeling blame is painful, a figurative purgatorial road to hell.

* * *

From clinical observation it would appear the abusers of other drugs — marijuana, cocaine, heroin, tranquilizers, codeine, demoral, morphine, barbiturates, amphetamines — behave in similarly mystifying ways.[2]

No one has classified drug addicts into alpha, beta, gamma, delta and epsilon categories the way Jellinek did alcoholics. We use the diagnostic categories of alcoholism to understand addiction to other drugs. On the whole it works.

Yes, pot is addictive. There are some heroin abusers who do not get hooked. Apparently there are even fewer crack cocaine smokers who do not become addicted.

* * *

Remember Fred the alcoholic and his exasperated wife, June? Well, then there's Max the paper boy who spends most of his paper money on marijuana. His parents don't know yet he's hooked; neither does he — except every once in a while he wonders about himself.

Thirty-nine-year-old Dora down the street has been taking tranquilizers for six years. Her physician is afraid to cut her off, lest she go into severe withdrawal. Truth to tell, as well as being his patient, she's also his customer and one who pays her bills. She tells herself it's OK, it's just medicine; it comes from the drugstore.

And Leroy. He alone of this bunch knows he's addicted. He's addicted so badly to crack he tries not to think about it. He's spent $41,347 this year on crack. Some of it was his, some was his sister's, and half was for his dad's retirement. His high is so high and so quick. Crack makes the norepinephrine and dopamine flow in his body. It is glorious! He says there's nothing like it, not even sex. Then the opponent process sets in, the deep depression and anhedonia (can't feel any pleasure). He's got to have relief, the instant relief that only comes from more crack, quickly purchased and smoked.

More than anyone realizes, there are straitjackets, blindfolds and little invisible clouds of purgatory scattered about the neighbor hood.

CAMELOT

All of these folk — Fred, Dora, the paper boy, and Leroy — have a similar problem with addiction. They are blind to the truth. They are out of touch with their drinking and drugging reality. Some psychotherapists call this the defense system or defense mechanisms. Substance abuse counselors usually just call it denial.

So much has been said about the objective side of denial — and I will have my say below — but here seems the place to speak about it subjectively, what it feels like, inside the addict's body, mind and soul.

Imagine, please, that we were at the theater watching Richard Harris in *Camelot*. He made us believe he was really King Arthur emerging from the mists of the Celtic dark ages, overlaid with fourteen centuries of Anglo-Saxon majesty. He was whacking about with Excalibur, his magical sword.

Guinevere, his bride-to-be, appeared. She had long golden hair and wanted to be rescued. She flirted with him and it worked. He bragged about his Camelot and tried his best to enchant her. He succeeded.

Just as the playwright intended, we adored them and loved watching him make her his queen.

Then from off stage the voice of Lancelot pierced like a spear, singing "Camelot". When he sang it, it had the same heart-quickening lilt as when Arthur sang it. Lancelot appeared and explained how he cleaved dragons in twain regularly and never lost in battle. His arrogance had charm! He was confident, courageous, skillful, manly and handsome. Instantly Arthur liked him. So did I. I could not help it. I did not want to help it.

Just a few scenes later Lancelot and Guinevere fell helplessly in love. At first it was purely poetic, chivalric love at a distance. It got more and more romantic. Then, behind the scenes somewhere, they finally made love.

King Arthur was betrayed. It was the downfall of Camelot. When it first began to dawn upon me I said to myself, "Oh, no! It can't be. It just can't be. Oh, no, they would never..."

I had seen it coming for several scenes and still did not want it to be true. And neither did anyone else in that theater. The play ended almost — but not quite — ambiguously so I could keep my denial if I had to.

The Camelot Factor is that strong "Oh, no!" impulse, that part of us that just does not want to see what is right in front of us. We want to avoid this truth at every level of our being. From the darkest part of the basement of our mind we simply refuse to see what we cannot bear to see, what we are most afraid to see.

As with Lancelot and Guinevere, seeing the truth nearly always involves loss of innocence. Literally and etymologically, if one is innocent one is not dangerous. We want to believe Lancelot and Guinevere are innocent.[3]

That "Oh, no!" feeling, multiplied many times over, is what it feels like to realize that one is addicted.

Alcoholics love ethanol (ethyl alcohol). I call her Ethyl. Alcoholics love Ethyl the way Lancelot loved Guinevere. Alcoholics love Ethyl so much they are afraid to lose her by admitting they are alcoholics. Potheads love Mary Jane (English translation of marijuana) so much they deny they are hooked. They are too scared to see.

In one form or another the King Arthur stories have stirred our souls since the late dark ages in Britain. This archetypal myth has promised adventure, noble quests, romance. It has made life hopeful, especially as it expanded into variations of medieval courtly love. The Knights of the Round Table pursuing the Holy Grail (supposedly the cup Jesus used at the Last Supper) inspired Thomas Malory's *The Holy Grail*, Wagner's *Parsifal*, T. H. White's *The Once and Future King*, Lerner and Lowe's *Camelot*, the movie *Excalibur*, Tennyson's *Morte d'Arthur* and *Idylls of the King*, Browning's *Fifane at the Fair* and scores of other tales and legends. Today "Camelot" often refers to the White House days of John and Jackie Kennedy and family. The myth has brought meaning to millions. It became a virtual religion in the sense that any myth which makes sense out of life, binds it together for us, is a religion.[4]

We saw Lancelot's love of Guinevere elevated, romanticized, virtually set among the stars. Without realizing it, Max the paper boy has done much the same with Mary Jane. He walks in the woods listening to his music through his earphones, communing with nature while smoking his pot. Cannabis has taken on sacramental proportions for him. Instead of "Take and eat, this is my body," it says, "Take and smoke, this is my soul."

* * *

And how do you tell if you are addicted? How do you tell if your son or daughter, or husband or wife, is addicted? Well, at first you cannot. You probably need to consult a professionally trained substance abuse counselor. The blindfold is at work on you too!

There are three major categories by which to diagnose addiction. Whether you use the *DSM-IV*,[5] the National Council on Alcoholism's

definition or many of the other professional definitions, or talk to an AA
member or an NA member, it still comes down to the same three things.
I call them "Oops", "Snafu" and "Invincible Ignorance".

OOPS

Oops means "Oops, I've done it again." It means loss of control in the
sense of loss of control of ingestion.[6] It does not mean loss of control of
behavior, like standing on the piano while wearing your golf shoes, singing, about to break into a buck and wing. That is loss of impulse control,
control over behavior. Any old drunk can lose control of impulse.

Oops comes after Dora has set limits on her drinking and tranquilizer
drugging. Neither her father nor her husband set those limits. Dora set
them for herself. She was only going to take three tranquilizers today, as
prescribed, but now at 4:30 this afternoon she's had seven or eight and
two vodkas with orange juice. She gets up to change the TV channel and
stumbles. "Oops," she says, and thinks, "There, I've done it again." She
feels remorse, but the remorse is dulled by the sedatives in her body. Once
again she has failed and once again she blames herself. But she holds on
tightly to the notion that she can control it next time!

Oops is the surprise that comes after Dora set controls for herself,
then could not live by them. She made a promise to herself and could not
keep it. She won't tell anyone. She is too ashamed.

The oops factor is insidious and sneaky. It is a chronic series of little
ambushes. The loss of control of ingestion that Fred experienced at first
was only about one time in twenty. After the first embarrassment he resolved to never let it happen again. And it didn't happen again for a couple
of months. Slowly it moved to 20 per cent of his drinking times, then
later 30 per cent and so on until now he loses control 85 per cent of the
time. But still, he can regain control sometimes, then delude himself he
has regained total control. What sticks in his mind is not percentages; it is
the proud memory of yesterday's control!

During the hangover, the experience of oops often deepens into depression, remorse and self-hatred. Fred still thinks he could stop but just
hasn't yet. He may swear off this morning. Later that afternoon he'll think,
"I'm no worse than anybody else. This worrying is silly. I'll just have two
drinks this afternoon — maybe three."

When June comes home at 7 p.m. she finds him passed out on the
sofa. He awakens with an "Oops" and says, "I must have fallen asleep
watching the news."

As oops magnifies it becomes increasingly terrifying, like having your brake pedal go flat to the floor as you approach a red light at a busy intersection. You can't stop! Still Fred and Dora continue to drink, insisting to themselves that they can stop next time.

The progression of the crack smokers leaves the alcoholics way behind. With crack you accelerate from zero to 150 mph in 4.3 seconds. With beverage alcohol it can take the better part of an hour for it to move through stomach to bloodstream to brain. Crack smoke takes a short cut, from lungs to blood to brain in less than five seconds.

SNAFU

"Snafu" is an old World War II term. British sailors said, "There's a spanner (a wrench) in the works." For American sailors, "snafu " was politely translated as, "situation normal, all fouled up." Few American sailors used the euphemism "fouled up." Snafu is when you sit on your glasses and break them, just when you have to sign this form and cannot find your pen. So you cannot write and could not see to write if you *had* a pen.

Fred is a hunter and every autumn he's been out in the Shenandoah Forest drinking whiskey and trying to shoot a deer. He never gets one. His drinking interferes with his hunting; "snafus" it.

Drinking and drugging snafu a lot of things: bank accounts, marriages, communications between a parent and children and homework for teenagers. Drinking can snafu the liver or the pancreas. It will snafu the ability to make love successfully. As Shakespeare said in *Macbeth*, "It provokes the desire, but it takes away the performance."

Drinking interferes with friendships. Old friends cannot keep pace with the progressive drinking and drugging. Such friends get dropped, or they drop the drinker.

The last snafu is the job, especially for men. It is such a source of pride and identity for them. More important, the job is the source of the stuff. No cash, no crack!

"Situation normal" for an addict is a life all fouled up.

* * *

INVINCIBLE IGNORANCE

Addicts who are abusing and alcoholics who are drinking are invincibly ignorant.[7] Anyone who is invincibly ignorant is not responsible for behavior rooted in that ignorance. Such ignorance is unconquerable, utterly impregnable. Anyone who has ever argued religion or politics has experienced it in an opponent. Almost every wife has suspected her husband of it on occasion. (And vice versa, every husband has suspected his wife of it.)

Alfred Lord Tennyson said it well: [8]

> Blind and naked Ignorance
> Delivers brawling judgements,
> Unashamed,
> On all things all day long.

Alcoholics deliver brawling judgments, all day long, when sober as well as when drunk. The invincible ignorance of the temporarily sober addict makes him forget the "oops" of last night. Fred will blindly go through today nakedly ignorant of what happened in yesterday's blackout. Max will invent an excuse to smoke pot again this afternoon.

True gamma alcoholics and drug addicts are all invincibly ignorant. But at the same time they are masters at persuading you to see things their way. It can feel the way it did when you were a kid and watched a magician make things disappear and reappear right in front of your eyes. Invincible ignorance is also a blindfold for family members, employers and friends.

Remember Fred and June? One day she came home and found him passed out. When she woke him he stood up and threw up. It was clear to her it was drunken vomiting. But when Fred got through with it, he convinced himself it was a virus going around the office. To prove it he made an appointment with Dr. Smith. So June began to doubt her own best judgment. Her husband was the magician now.

Six weeks later Fred staggered home five hours late from a "business" meeting (at the club). He was in a blackout, a state of alcohol-induced amnesia, not to be confused with being passed out. The clinical name for a blackout is a palimpsest, information *biochemically* misfiled in the brain. Fred would not remember this the next day. June didn't know he was in a blackout, nor did she know what a blackout was.

June was worried, then relieved to see him, then furious. They had words. He refused to eat his scorched dinner and staggered off to bed mumbling. She heard the words, "Goddamned (something mumbled) bitch!"

Next morning he came to (as opposed to waking up) with only the vaguest notions about last night. He could not remember leaving the club, looked in the driveway to see if the car was there and had no memory of what he said to June. Meanwhile June was in the kitchen drinking coffee and wondering if she really was a bitch. Fred left for work without even trying to penetrate the arctic blast of air coming from the kitchen. That evening, while he was on his second highball, Fred heard in stunned disbelief about his calling her a bitch.

By the time Fred got through listening carefully, then explaining carefully, he had explained it all away. It was just like the magician when June was a little girl. Yesterday you heard it. Today you didn't. Fred was out of touch with reality.

He is invincibly ignorant. June is getting that way too.

June does not want anyone to think her husband is an alcoholic. It would seem a source of embarassment and shame, a reflection upon her. She would fear being even more a failure as a wife. June reacts as I did when it occured to me Lancelot and Guinevere's adultery was bringing down Camelot, castle and all. I said to myself, "Oh, no! It can't be; it just can't." June fears Fred's drinking will destroy the castle of their home.

Fred and June still attend church and take their children to Sunday school. If you ask what they believe in they will tell you the God of the Bible, much as the Reverend Mr. Goodcastle explains Him. But a subtle spiritual change is occurring.

Fred is following Ethyl, like some modern goddess, into his invisible purgatory. June is not far behind. While Fred has found a new god, she is trying to *be* God. She is obsessed with his drinking. She tries to be everywhere to find his booze (omnipresence), know everything about his drinking (omniscience) and control his drinking (omnipotence).

The road to recovery must be found in a humble, spiritual relation to a kind and loving, yet tough and strong God. Fred and June are traveling in the opposite direction. As with all those who are invincibly ignorant, their ignorance is unconquerable — for now.

ENDNOTES

1. *The Disease Concept of Alcoholism* by E.M. Jellinek, New Haven, 1960, page 37.

2. Although the lion's share of scientific research is on males with alcohol problems there is some confirmation of this. 'Genetic Models in the Study of Alcoholism' in the May 1993 issue of *Journal of Progress in Neuro-*

Psychopharmacology & Biological Psychiatry, pages 345-61, finds evidence that genes may determine to some extent drug-seeking behaviors for cocaine and opiates also.

3.   Robert Penn Warren said in *Brother to Dragons* "The recognition of complicity is the beginning of innocence," with a meaning counter to our first reading's impression.

4.   From the Latin verb *religo,* to tie on, to fasten behind, to bind back together. By definition whatever myths we believe in to "get it all to-gether" to make sense out of our lives, constitute our religion. Interest-ingly, the Bible does not consider itself "religious" and rarely uses the word. When it does refer to "religion" it means something wicked.

5.   *Diagnostic and Statistical Manual Number IV* of the American Psychiatric Association.

6.   Ingestion could be by mouth (smoking or drinking), by a vein, by injection into a muscle, by inhaling through the nose, or even by enema.

7.   The term is from medieval moral theology. As St. Thomas Aquinas put it, "A man is not blamed for negligence if he is ignorant of what he cannot know: therefore such ignorance is called invincible, because it cannot be overcome by effort." S.T. I, 2, quæst. lxxvi, art. 2 as quoted on page 40, *The Elements of Moral Theology*, by R. C. Mortimer, London, 1947.

8.   *Merlin and Vivien*, line 662.

Chapter III
Willpower

"But what about willpower?" you ask.

Addiction is a disease of the will. The will has lost its power. As one very wise recovering alcoholic told me, "You see, if I get into an argument with a drink, the drink will win." He went on to explain: "That is, if I stay alone with myself and argue. However, if I take that argument to an AA meeting and share it, we [the AA group] can do what I cannot do alone. 'We' win that argument."

The addicted will cannot see past itself, its own narcissism, its own self-absorption.

A number of impressive, seminal thinkers of our Western civilization have cast serious doubt on whether anyone has a free will. St. Paul said[1] "I do not understand my own actions. For I do not do what I want, but I do the very thing I hate... I can will what is right, but I cannot do it." The Latin poet Ovid said[2] "I see the right and approve it too: condemn the wrong yet the wrong pursue." Their contemporary, an author of the Jewish *Talmud*, said "The inclination to evil—it is that which turns a man into the enemy of himself, at war with himself, as though he were a thing torn apart by contending armies, making null the good he intends."

St. Augustine of Hippo was the first Christian theologian to develop a doctrine of predestination. He believed this was essential because of the Fall of Adam. As a consequence, he concluded, we are all *non posse non pecarre*, incapable of refraining from sin. He believed we were too bound up with ourselves to reach upward to God.

Martin Luther initiated the Protestant Reformation. Seminal in his thinking was his work, *The Bondage of the Will*, a lengthy denial of free will. His contemporary, John Calvin, expanded predestination theology based on his conviction that the human will was so bound up with itself it was incapable of making a choice for God.

Without understanding their assumptions about human nature and its bondage, it is easy to consign Augustine, Luther and Calvin to a trash bin of mechanistic determinism. Possibly the two greatest Twentieth Century Protestant theologians were Karl Barth and Paul Tillich. Both agree with Augustine, Luther and Calvin that we do not have free will; rather our wills need to be set free under God.

The two great depth psychologists, Sigmund Freud and Carl Jung, taught that the conscious will was largely dominated by the "unconscious" forces which largely determine our so-called "decisions."

Whatever else one might want to say of these thinkers, they all studied human nature and concluded that the human will was far more bound than free.

I agree with the above thinkers that the human will is largely in bondage at the beginning of our lives. Growing up means becoming free through growth, often a painful process. Some grow more than others. Still others never grow up at all.

With addiction to alcohol or other drugs, the human bondage becomes tighter, even more confining. Like those Dante described in his *Purgatorio*, we are in bondage to that which we chose. The thief is in bondage to stealing, the liar is in bondage to lying. The alcoholic is in bondage to the alcohol s/he chose, the crack smoker even more so.

*   *   *

Near the end of Chapter One I said, "In order to make my case for spirituality as all-encompassing, I must discuss the three dimensions of addiction [physical, mental and spiritual] at length. Now I press further into this and ask the reader's patience.

Addiction is a threefold disease. The will has been contaminated physically, mentally and spiritually.

THE BODY

World-class alcoholism researcher Dr. George E. Vaillant says that in one way alcohol addiction can be compared to tuberculosis. Not everyone who is exposed to the tubercle bacillus catches tuberculosis. Not every heavy whisky drinker becomes addicted to it. Addiction to beverage alcohol is a habit-forming process. Possibly a label should be attached to each whisky bottle saying, "Caution, may be habit forming." Vaillant compared the continuous heavy drinker to the drunk man driving a junky old car with burned-out taillights, bald tires and bad brakes. You cannot predict for sure *when* the calamity will occur, but you are pretty certain it will.[3] The more the drinker drinks, the more likely is addiction.

Once addiction has grasped the drinker, the adaptations in cell metabolism change the body forever, in a process somewhat analogous to a cucumber cured in pickle brine. The pickle can never return to its pristine cucumber state.

As an old Asian proverb has it, "First the man takes the drink, then the drink takes the drink and finally the drink takes the man."

Some children of alcoholics are anxious in a social setting. Their brain waves show this. Dr. Donald Goodwin and others have discovered that if you give them one ounce of alcohol their brain wave activity relaxes.[4] They have a problem with dopamine and serotonin balance. At first booze brings their serotonin up to a normal level, then above normal, then later plunges it below normal. It is a double hook. The opiate receptor gene is activated, then it experiences a sharp withdrawal. Initially "they drink to feel good [normal] and then later drink to stop feeling bad".[5]

We do not know why the brains of these offspring of alcoholics function differently, making life in general more difficult. Presumably it is something they inherited.

Other studies by some of the same researchers prove that sons of alcoholics taken away from their parents just after birth and raised in non-alcoholic families are still four times as likely to be alcoholic as anyone else.[6] Surprisingly, however, if they stay home with their alcoholic parents the risk isn't any worse.

Other researchers[7] have demonstrated that a significant portion of Asians have "an atypical ALDH2 gene." After the metabolism of alcohol to acetaldehyde, this anomaly prevents its metabolism to acetic acid at a point which makes these drinkers sick. Acetaldehyde backs up in the system. It is a chemical some experts have described as similar to formaldehyde. This explains why this minority of Asians have a painful reaction to alcohol not unlike the one you would have if you took Antabuse, then drank! My point is that different people — sometimes whole cultures of people — react differently to alcohol ingestion. It is clear that the interaction of acetaldehyde, dopamine and serotonin in the bodies of alcoholics and addicts differs from the interaction in non-addicted people.

The scientific community agrees[8] that "Twin, family and adoption studies have demonstrated that people can inherit a vulnerability to strong drink. But whether it's a specific vulnerability to alcohol or a more general addictive proclivity has not been established." Eliot Marshall says "dopamine is the chief neurotransmitter in the brain's 'pleasure center'." [9]

The hunt for the demon gene(s) as a cause of alcoholism continues. In 1990 a study claiming to have found and identified this gene as the dopamine D2 receptor gene was published.[10] Other genes or alleles may be complicit in the process. The senior dopamine D2 investigator, Ernest P. Noble, continues his research.[11] J. R. Volpicelli and colleagues believe "Endorphins are partially responsible."[12]

The D3 dopamine receptor has been implicated "to be a central factor in cocaine use" by Dr. George F. Koob of the National Institute of Drug Abuse.[13] Other researchers are working with animal studies and can produce addiction in rats and monkeys by manipulation of their brain chemistry.[14]

Many researchers are convinced we must abandon " 'one-gene one-disorder' thinking".[15] Eliot Marshall says we must go beyond single-gene etiology and utilize the art of computerized multivariate analysis to scan the whole genome. This will be difficult and will take a while. He quotes a fish pool analogy story told by David Cox of Stanford University.[16] The 'one-gene one-disorder' method is

> like using a small net to snag a fish out of a pool, when it would be better to drain the pool and collect all the fish from the bottom. Doing whole-genome scans—though more time consuming—is like draining the pool...Some investigators would still rather take their chances at "winning the lotto"—hitting one gene that is responsible.

In summary, the brain chemistry of alcoholics is different. Social drinkers and alcoholics do not drink on a level playing field. Human DNA codes differ.

Just as some people have allergic reactions to ragweed and poison ivy, so other people metabolize acetaldehyde with great discomfort. One person *appreciates* serotonin more than another, finds more relief from it.

An alcoholic's reaction to alcohol is different from that of a social drinker. To expect otherwise is equivalent to expecting someone with a wooden leg to compete evenly with able-bodied people in the 100-yard dash.

As yet, medicine cannot cure addiction. Some scientists hope for a cure by genetic engineering, tampering with DNA codes. Many, including myself, are not sanguine that we ever will find a cure. And, if we could engineer it away, what else might we stir up? We have an unsolved mystery in the addicted body.

The only hope for recovery is in accepting the addicted body as it is and finding strength elsewhere to cut addicts free from their straitjackets. This will take enormous power. It must come from another place, a spiritual dimension.

When we do not know what else to do, most of us pray. The Serenity Prayer fits this enigma with precision.

> God, grant me the serenity to accept the things I cannot change,
> courage to change the things I can
> and wisdom to know the difference.

Recovering addicts have accepted that they cannot change their bodies. The habit has taken permanent hold upon them inside their very body cells. Their hope must come from learning to live with this fact day in and day out, "one day at a time." Obviously this takes a lot of courage. Since they cannot change their bodies, their minds and souls must change through daily prayer and meditation, going to AA meetings, talking with their sponsors and immersion into the full power of the AA fellowship. They learn to gain strength from others in a spiritual community.

Yes, the disease of addiction inhabits the body, but the best treatment for the body comes from a spiritual source.

THE MIND

Understanding how an addict thinks is somewhere between difficult and impossible. AA describes alcoholism as "cunning and baffling".[17] Some people ask recovering alcoholics to explain their thinking, as if they understood themselves. They work hard in their meetings at explaining themselves to each other, but their understanding of themselves is limited, as they are often the first to admit. When they try to explain themselves to non-addicts they often give up in frustration.

Psychiatrist George E. Vaillant of Harvard has done impressive, objective alcoholism research which supports the AA position. Vaillant's analysis of the Grant studies and the Core City studies, begun in Boston in the late 1930's, covers a "proscriptive" 40-year period, following 204 healthy Ivy League college sophomores and 456 healthy inner-city teenage boys from Boston. With proper statistical procedures he concluded there were only two reliable predictors of alcoholism: inheritance and ethnic background. He has discredited classical Freudian theory in treating alcoholism.[18] Invalidating the theory of the "alcoholic personality", he said,

"It was difficult to discard the illusion that...unhappy childhoods, membership in multiproblem families, depression and anxiety" were not "major etiological consideration(s)".[19] In other words, people do not become addicted because they have low self-esteem. They get low self-esteem as a *result* of addictive drinking or drugging.

Freudian psychiatry assumed, *a priori*,[20] that addiction is not itself the disease, but merely a symptom of a deeper, underlying personality disorder. This "addictive personality" was thought to have originated in a depressed, unhappy childhood; alcoholics were trapped at the "oral" stage and "arrested" in latent homosexuality.

Freud missed the obvious by identifying addiction as secondary rather than primary. If depression causes addiction, then depression is primary and addiction secondary. Truth is, addiction is primary and often causes depression, anxiety, guilt, shame and other complications.[21]

Unfortunately, some Freudians continue to miss the obvious.[22] Jerome Levin, a Freudian psychologist, preserves the *a priori* error. He first misrepresents his fellow psychoanalyst, saying, "Vaillant also argues that adult alcoholics retrospectively falsify the degree of pathology in their childhood environments." No! Vaillant says psychotherapists manipulate their alcoholic patients to describe their childhood environments so as to meet the psychotherapist's preconceived diagnostic categories. Levin tries to dismiss the distinguished Harvard professor's research with: "Vaillant's data cannot be argued away, but his interpretation of it is not persuasive."[23]

Freudian theory is a construct, a non-scientific theory constructed before approaching the facts. It is like a parable, to be taken seriously but not literally.

It can be helpful or unhelpful.

It can be helpful as a widely understood myth like *Camelot*. The validity of *Camelot* as history is questionable, to say the least, yet *Camelot* is useful in revealing truths about ourselves. As Freudian thought has lost utility among research psychologists, its use by historians, playwrights, screenwriters and novelists has increased. It is an organizing myth, a story around which to construct a believable plot.

Although Vaillant classifies himself as a Freudian, he finds dangers in treating addiction with traditional Freudian therapy.[24] He explains that psychiatric misunderstanding of the causes of alcoholism can make an alcoholic patient worse, creating problems from the past which never existed.

James O'Neill, one of the original subjects in the Grant studies, personifies this. He was recovering very well from alcoholism in AA years after the original study when Vaillant met him. The original records in the archives of O'Neill's early life prove he came from a very healthy, happy home. Yet O'Neill was convinced he did not love his mother and had contracted other mental morbidities in childhood. O'Neill was still suffering pathology he had "caught" from his Freudian psychiatrist.

While psychoanalysis has not been helpful in explaining the causes of addiction, it is helpful in explaining why alcoholics are invincibly ignorant.

Fortunately some Freudians are openminded. Dr. Harry Tiebout, a classical Freudian psychiatrist and an early consultant to AA, did impressive work in explaining the mental defenses of alcoholics.[25] Dr. Tiebout described what I call the compliance/defiance syndrome. (See Figures 1 and 2 below.) It is the blindfold, an unconscious denial of reality. Underneath a conscious and compliant willingness to admit "I'm an addict," is a whole set of defiant thoughts and passions outside of conscious awareness. These unconscious passions are tightly held and grandiose. Consciously the alcoholic is frightened about his drinking but unconsciously he ignores and "overrides" this fear. Alcoholics can drink until their dying day in unconscious defiance and infantile grandiosity. It is as if deeper, primary process thinking, down in the basement of the mind, is holding a pep rally to win this contest. The lower, primitive brain has become "hooked" and demands sedation. Now!

Imagine an adolescent male forbidden to masturbate, frightened by admonitions it will drive him insane, give him pimples and damn him to hell. Yet his sexual drives are in full strength and they *will* have their way. Willpower that lives "upstairs" in the mind cannot compete with this primitive drive. The alcohol, heroin or crack addicted mind is driven by forces from below which are just as powerful as adolescent sexual passions.

Normal, healthy life for a non-addicted person is what Karl Menninger referred to in a book of the same name as *The Vital Balance*.[26] He got the idea from Freud.[27] To be fully alive is to have vitality! This means living between the two forces, between primary and secondary processes. It is a carefully crafted tightrope walk between civilization's laws, good manners and constraints from above and the primitive, growling animal passions from below. Most people walk this tightrope largely unaware of what a clever trick they are performing.

When people are "mentally ill" and go for treatment by psychoanalysts or ego psychologists, the therapy is largely a matter of understanding (analyzing) this balance.

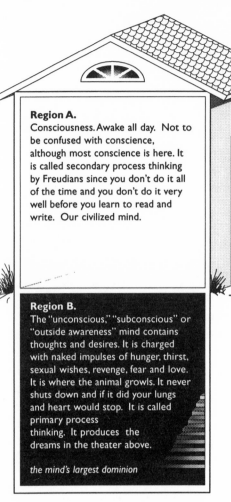

Region A.
Consciousness. Awake all day. Not to be confused with conscience, although most conscience is here. It is called secondary process thinking by Freudians since you don't do it all of the time and you don't do it very well before you learn to read and write. Our civilized mind.

Region B.
The "unconscious," "subconscious" or "outside awareness" mind contains thoughts and desires. It is charged with naked impulses of hunger, thirst, sexual wishes, revenge, fear and love. It is where the animal growls. It never shuts down and if it did your lungs and heart would stop. It is called primary process thinking. It produces the dreams in the theater above.

the mind's largest dominion

Figure I. THE COMPLIANCE/DEFIANCE SYNDROME A   (non-addicted)
A construct picture of the "mind".

It is important to understand that in figure 1 we are describing a healthy person who has no problems with addiction.

Let us assume the above mind has inherited the addictive receptor genomes or other similar characteristics which give it a voracious appetite for alcohol, marijuana, heroin, tranquilizers, amphetamines, barbiturates, sleeping pills or cocaine. The chemical has been producing its magic across the receptor sites long enough for the body to get hooked. Natural body mood changers and pain killers such as dopamine, serotonin and norepinephrine are released, bind to receptors, or inhibited at times and in places unnatural. As the "upper" or "downer" euphoria juices recede, old pains and anxieties rebound with a vengeance.

Nothing less than total surrender of these unconscious forces will result in a beginning of recovery.

From this basement headquarters of the mind, all sorts of defenses are fashioned:

A. **Comparison,** as in "Well, I'm not that bad yet." The addict can always find someone worse off, more degenerate. Comparison is the opposite of identification. Identification with other recovering alcoholics is what happens when Fred goes to the meeting, says "I'm Fred and I'm an alcoholic" and really means it.

The very identity itself is under attack. The work of absorbing the term "addict" or "alcoholic" into oneself is no small accomplishment.

All of us, including alcoholics and addicts, prefer to see ourselves as kind, considerate and, most of all, not dangerous (innocent). Most of us go about parading more innocence than we have. We trust in our own righteousness and try to appear before our fellows as morally correct. If I am asked to say, "My name is Bob and I'm an alcoholic," I am asked to say something abrasively painful and insulting. It is not the way I choose to understand myself.

I know that you know that if I say I am alcoholic, it is tantamount to my saying "and I've also spent considerable time being selfish, drunken, narcissistic, unkind, forgetful, irresponsible, deceitful and generally dangerous to have around."

If I have strong enough ego defenses in the basement I will just marshal them, puff myself up and (in effect) announce, "I will not be an alcoholic. I don't care how many dopamine genome receptor sites I have. I will not be an alcoholic. I'm not *that* bad!" I will defy reality itself.

Or I might develop a strategy that appears different to you because I wear a passive-aggressive mask. I will adopt a stance of compliance, possibly admitting I'm some kind of an alcoholic (a "weekend" alcoholic, for instance), as if that made any difference. It has an "if you say so" flavor to it. The basement voices are still singing "drink, drink...", but I tune them out. When asked about my alcoholism, I'll say "I don't know" a lot. And I won't know. My psyche will see to that. And it won't even bother me.

B. Projection occurs as Fred projects angry blame out of himself onto June: "Hell, with a wife like you, anybody would have to drink," then picks up his drink as if he were as innocent as a newborn child. Often he gets away with it. As Vernon Johnson pointed out,[30] "The

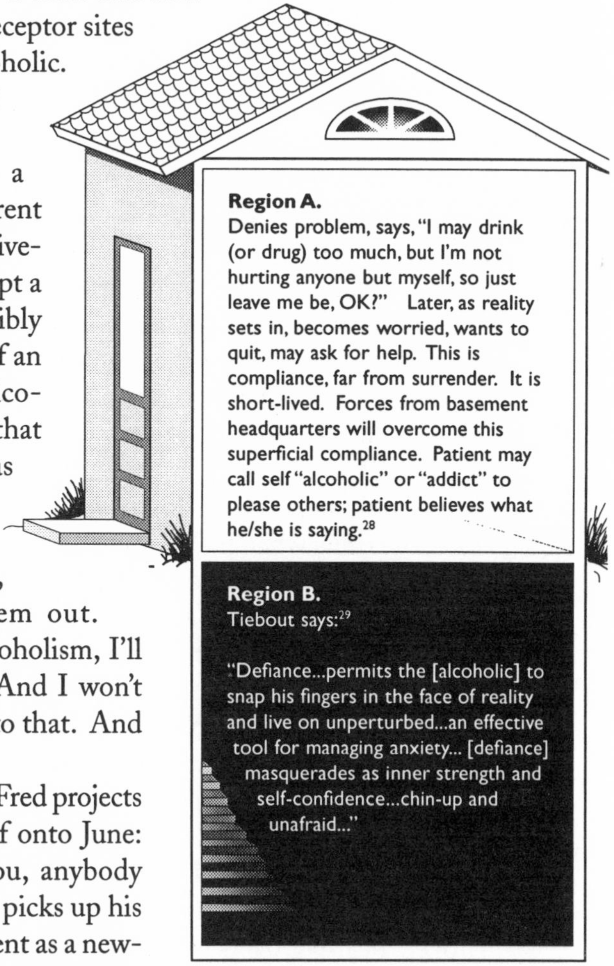

Region A.
Denies problem, says, "I may drink (or drug) too much, but I'm not hurting anyone but myself, so just leave me be, OK?" Later, as reality sets in, becomes worried, wants to quit, may ask for help. This is compliance, far from surrender. It is short-lived. Forces from basement headquarters will overcome this superficial compliance. Patient may call self "alcoholic" or "addict" to please others; patient believes what he/she is saying.[28]

Region B.
Tiebout says:[29]

"Defiance...permits the [alcoholic] to snap his fingers in the face of reality and live on unperturbed...an effective tool for managing anxiety... [defiance] masquerades as inner strength and self-confidence...chin-up and unafraid..."

Figure 2 THE COMPLIANCE/DEFIANCE SYNDROME B (addicted)

more hateful the alcoholic unconsciously sees himself to be, the more he will come to see himself surrounded by hateful people." The more he can blame others, the less he needs to look at himself!

Projection can also be passive. I'll eschew assertion and collect sympathy, all the while manipulating others to say how unkind my wife is. I'll just stand by looking concerned and understanding, letting others do the blaming. My facade of innocence shines in the sunlight. If I'm good enough at it, once in a while I'll even fool a seasoned substance-abuse counselor.

C. Blackouts. Fred called June a bitch, yet was unaware of it next morning. What he cannot remember, he cannot monitor in his behavior. What he cannot monitor, he cannot change. It he does not know how much pain he causes his wife, he can't change what he does not know about.

D. Rationalization. The worse things get, the more remorse and shame Fred feels. The worse Fred feels, the more he thinks. The better he thinks, the less he has to feel. The more he thinks, the further out of touch with his feelings he gets. (As Leroy the crack addict described it, "You can't feel what you feel.") So, Fred thinks! He thinks to himself, "Well, it was late and I am way overworked. I had nothing on my stomach and besides they were late serving dinner. Of course those martinis got the best of me. What's the big deal?" Dora rationalizes when she thinks to herself, "My tranquilizers are only medicine, so even if I do take more than I'm supposed to it's legal and medical, so I'm innocent of drug abuse."

E. Minimizing. As any highway patrolman can tell you, everyone says the same thing when pulled over and asked, "Sir, have you been drinking?" The all say, "Well, just a couple, officer." Did you ever know anyone to say, "Well, let's see, back at the tavern, about 5:30, I had those three Manhattans, then before dinner two more at the restaurant, then there was that Chardonnay with the meal, two glasses as I remember, and then, oh, yes, we had two Benedictine and brandies with a cigar after dinner"?

F. Euphoric recall is the memory of the high. But it is not simple cognitive memory, as in remembering that 2 x 3 = 6. No, your whole body remembers, as it does with a marvelous sexual memory with someone you once loved. You still have the bodily echoes of it. It is also called a somatic memory.

Broken-hearted lovers understand this. You went to tell him it was over; that was what your willpower said, what your best judgment said. But once you got there, you got to understanding and forgiving one another. Against all of your best judgment, you wound up in bed together. Willpower got thrown on the floor, right beside your clothes!

Cocaine and heroin addicts compare their drug highs with sexual orgasms. It is the only analogy they know that is strong enough. They insist the drug is better than sex.

As you read this, somewhere, not too far away from you, Leroy has been up and smoking crack for over 72 hours. No pauses, no sleep. He is almost out of crack. Three more pipefuls is all he has. In spite of all of his experience for the past seventy-one and a half hours, he is still chasing that high he hasn't had for three days. That memory is euphoric recall.

In summary, the psychological bondage of addiction seduces the will so that it does not even *want* to resist. "I'm not that bad," it convinces itself. "What's the big deal? I'm not hurting anyone but myself." Reality is that far gone. As in a blacksmith shop of old, addicts thoughts are heated, hammered, bent about and twisted — rationalized — until they listen only to the beckoning of their drug.

As Tiebout put it, the "unconscious mind rejects through its capacity for defiance and grandiosity what its conscious mind perceives. Hence, realistically, the individual *is frightened by his drinking and at the same time is prevented from doing anything about it* by the unconscious activity which can and does ignore or override the conscious mind." (emphasis mine)

Vernon Johnson says it this way: "The patient's chief fear is that his presentation of himself will be destroyed...[that he] will...[be] taken apart or 'cut up' [saying] 'What are you trying to do — murder me?'"

Reason and persuasion, willpower and moral exhortations, talking cures and behavior modification usually fail to penetrate invincible ignorance. As with the bodily disease of addiction, the defenses of the mind are more likely to yield to spiritual therapy. Episcopal priest Vernon Johnson believes the objective is not to blast away defenses but to find a way the alcoholic can "see and accept enough reality."[31] This can happen only if this truth "is presented to him in a receivable form."[32]

The spiritual route of defense penetration is *graceful honesty*. Graciousness and love are not enough. Neither are honesty and truth. It will take a lot of *both* truth and grace.

Graciousness, kindness, love and forgiveness devoid of encounter with reality are perceived by alcoholics as permission to continue in their old ways. But brutal honesty alone is not only unkind; it is ineffective. If the confrontation is not graceful and sensitive, the basement of the mind will immediately erect new defenses.

Since spiritual therapy is so difficult to explain, let alone apply, I shall try it two different ways: the biblical way and the AA way.

BIBLICAL SPIRITUALITY

The biblical way I prefer is a short description of Jesus of Nazareth, whom Christians call the Christ, by the author of the Fourth Gospel.[33] To "John"[34] Jesus personifies both grace and truth. He is not only intensely loving and compassionate, he also has the lowdown on all of us! Sometimes he confronts us with it.

An extremely embarrassed woman is dragged before him, caught in the act of adultery.[35] He instantly forgives her, although he tells her to stop it, then confronts her accusers with their self-righteousness. In a similar situation[36] he is at a dinner party at the home of Simon the Pharisee. The other guests are shocked at the behavior of a whore from the streets. The scene is quite sensuous. She is in tears, kissing the feet of Jesus, wiping the tears from his feet with her hair. Not only is Jesus sympathetic to the whore, he decides to use her love as an example for the other guests and his disciples. He explains how she is capable of such love only because she has experienced much forgiveness.

Paul Tillich elaborated on this scene, explaining why the righteous "cannot help us," because they are "hard and self-assured." They cannot understand the woman's pain. They misunderstand the plea in her heart. They "believe they do not need much [forgiveness]".[37] (The most common complaint of addicts and alcoholics is not being understood.)

Some psychotherapists remain emotionally aloof from their patients, creating this "hard and self-assured" shell to protect themselves. They cannot penetrate an addict's defenses![38]

When you think about it, Jesus got away with a lot of confrontation before they killed him. He predicted Peter would deny him and Peter told him that was impossible.[39] He told his followers that if they did not feed the hungry, clothe the naked and take in the homeless they were no followers of his.[40] He confronted the greedy,[41] the judgmental,[42] the unkind and the bitter.[43] He was loving and kind, honest and confrontive, "full of grace and truth."

AA SPIRITUALITY

The AA spiritual equivalent is called tough love. While good AA is amazingly patient and loving, it is also hard as nails.

For years I have sent patients to AA from Alcohol Safety Action Programs, mental hospitals, my private practice and treatment centers. These patients have often been resentful and taken out their frustrations on AA members in the meetings. I am constantly surprised at the patience of these AA members. They welcome the wayward with kindness, yet move on with what they are doing. They remember they must not "spend too much time on any one alcoholic" because they might "deny some other an opportunity."[44] They know the goal is "ego collapse at depth,"[45] that each alcoholic must hit his or her own bottom. The patients are often arrogant, sometimes even belligerent. The old-timers look at each other and shake their heads. They remind each other, "You can carry the message but you can't carry the alcoholic." They remember they are looking into a mirror of what they once were.

Later they may be awakened in the middle of the night by someone to whom they gave their telephone number. If the other end sounds sober they will listen and talk. If not, they will politely say goodnight.

Tough love or grace-and-truth love are spiritual powers accessed from elsewhere. There is more strength to the equation than the wits of the therapist or the individual AA member.

Recovering alcoholics and addicts believe they have a mission to "carry the message." They believe they have a strong backup. His name is "HP", Higher Power, or "God as we understood Him."[46]

Spiritual power can penetrate the mind's defenses as no other power can. If the substance-abuse counselor is not in recovery it is wise to have someone nearby who is to mediate this HP spirituality.

THE SOUL

Vernon Johnson pointed out that from the very start the alcoholic develops a spiritual relationship with alcohol.[47] He emphasized in italics that it *will carry through the rest of his life.*

It is a trust relationship, a faith relationship. From the beginning, Fred learned to trust his whisky: 1. It makes him feel good all over his body, right now! 2. It works every time, as nothing else does. If it rains on his parade, Ethyl is still there. 3. Fred is in charge. He controls the dosage. Two beers are better than one and liquor is quicker. Or, as a nice lady in AA once put it, "If some is good, more is better and too much is never enough!"

Fred's alcohol has become the most important thing in his life, the thing he goes to sleep dreaming about, the thing he labors to purchase, more important than his wife or even his life. His drug has become his god and *he does not realize it.*

He loses his capacity to cope with normal, everyday anxiety. Theologians call it existential anxiety, the kind of anxiety that "goes with the territory" of being human. It is incurable.[48]

As Sheldon Kopp put it, "There's no way to get it all straight. Mistakes are inevitable."[49] Therefore some guilt happens — inevitable, existential guilt. This causes anxiety. Existential anxiety always accompanies responsibility. Other sources of existential anxiety are human loneliness and human insatiability (we never get enough of whatever it is we think we want, or if we do get it, we don't want it anymore). We all have anxiety just because we are mortal. Not only will we all die, but things keep happening to remind us how fragile we are.

The greatest number of us cope spiritually with existential anxiety, whether we belong to a church or not. Spirituality is whatever source of strength we use to cope with such questions as: Why am I here? Do I count? For how much? Do I have a place in the sun that is mine? Do I have a calling, a vocation? What is my destiny? Is there any chance of life after death? Anyway, is there a God? Does God hear my prayers? Can I be forgiven by Whatever is out there or up there or dwelling here in me?

Once the drug becomes a god, the addict's spiritual resources for coping with everyday anxiety ebb away. This is why recovering addicts must find some kind of Higher Power. They have lost their old familiar god, booze or crack cocaine, and need another to take its place. The attempt to live without any Higher Power is tried by some, rarely with any success.

In the medieval world, an ignorant world compared to ours, yet a world in some ways more spiritually sophisticated than ours, Dante pointed out something we miss today.

I must use a word I fear will cause some to misunderstand me completely. That word is "damnation." I use the word figuratively and existentially, not literally. I do not believe in a sadistic, child-abuser Higher Power who needs to torture his wayward children in a fiery furnace down in a dark basement. Such a Higher Power takes on the monstrous attributes of Jeffrey Dahmer!

Damnation is the isolation that comes from seeking our own will rather than the will of God.

We are most "damned" when we are cut off from those we love, from our spiritual resources, from our co-workers, from our extended families, from society and ultimately from our God Himself. Addicts get what they think they want and become isolated, in bondage to what they chose. They are desperately lonely, damned to isolation. They have only themselves and they hate themselves.

They only think they are free. Yet of all men and women, who is in greater bondage? Whatever free will they once had is now gone to hell in a handbasket.

* * *

Theologian Paul Tillich described existential anxiety as "the basic insecurity of human existence."[50] In the early 1950's he returned to his native Germany and was shocked and saddened by what he saw in the faces of his countrymen as a result of their complicity in the Holocaust. (Tillich had made an ethical decision to leave Germany in the early 1930's. Although the Holocaust had not yet begun, the Christian churches, both Roman Catholic and Protestant, had abdicated their moral and ethical authority to Hitler.)[51]

He described the faces of his compatriots as "shaped by burdens too heavy to be carried...with denial of guilt, self-excuse and accusation of others, self pity and self hate."

Tillich explained their existential predicament as an ineluctable tension "between the desire of being healed and the fear of being healed."

However, amidst this Teutonic purgatory he found hope. He found a few who had been healed, who were "whole in spite of their disruption" and "serene in spite of their sorrow."

He described their change in attitude as spiritual, an act of faith which definitely does "not appeal to our will power." The cost of this change is more than the unaided human will can pay. The price is an acceptance of our darker nature.

This darker nature of his compatriots was only partially hidden. Tillich described them:

> Split, contradicting themselves, disgusted and despairing about themselves, hateful of themselves and therefore hostile towards everybody else, afraid of life, burdened with guilt feelings, accusing and excusing themselves, fleeing from others into loneliness.[52]

It will already be apparent to some readers this also describes addicts and alcoholics before recovery. Other readers may still find therapeutic spirituality a bit baffling. For them I will do my best to shed more light in chapters Four through Eight.

The saving faith of the recovering Germans came only with *surrender*. Tillich said this "faith means being grasped by a power that is greater than we are, a power that shakes us and turns us, and transforms and heals us."

ENDNOTES

1. Romans 7:15, 19.

2. *Metamorphoses.*

3. Dr. Vaillant speaking at the Virginia Association of Alcohol and Drug Abuse Counselors conference in Charlottesville, Virginia, March 20, 1995.

4. Goodwin, Donald W., Genetic Influences in Alcoholism, *Avd. Intern Med.* 32 283 298, 1987, page 291. Propping P, Kruger J, Mark N, "Genetic Disposition to Alcoholism," *Human Genetics,* Vol 59:51-59, 1981. Propping, P, Kruger, J, Janah, A, Effect of Alcohol on Genetically Determined Variants of the Normal EEG. *Psychiatry Research,* Vol. 2:85-90, 1980.

5. Goodwin, ibid, page 291. Parenthetic explanation mine.

6. Goodwin, Donald W.: "Genetic Factors in the Development of Alcoholism," *Psychiatric Clinics of North America.* Vol 9: 427-433, 1986. Goodwin, Donald W., Schulsinger, F, Moller, N, *et al*: "Drinking Problems in Adopted and Nonadopted Sons of Alcoholics." *Archives of General Psychiatry,* Vol 31: 164-169, 1974.

7. *Journal of Pharmacogenetics,* April 1992.

8. Marshall, Eliot, *Science* Vol 264. 17 June 1994, page 1696.

9. Ibid.

10. *Journal of the American Medical Association,* Vol 263; 2055-2060, 1990. (Blum, Noble & Sheridan).

11. *Scientific American,* "The Gene That Rewards Alcoholism," Ernest P. Noble, March/April 1996, pages 52-61.

12. Volpicelli, J.R., Berg, B.J. and Watson, N.T., *The Pharmacology of Alcohol Abuse,* H.R. Kanzler, ed., Springer, 1995, Chapter 8, page 172.

13. *The Counselor,* a publication of The National Association of Alcoholism and Drug Abuse Counselors, March/April 1996, page 4.

14. Collins, M.A. et al, *J of Neurochem,* Vol. 55, No. 5, 1990; Myers, R.D. et al, *Brain Research Bulletin,* Vol. 22, pp. 899-911, 1989; Cashaw, J.L. et al, *Journal of Neuroscience Res.* 18:497-503 (1987); Clow, A. *Neuropharmacology,* Vol. 22, No. 4, pp 563-565, 1983; Duncan, C. C. et al, *Alcohol,* Vol. 8. pp. 87-90, 1991; Privette, T.H. et al, *Alcohol,* Vol.5, pp.147-152, 1988; Myers, R.D. et al, *Pharmacology Biochemistry & Behavior,* Vol. 16, pp. 827-836, 1982. See bibliography under senior author's name for more detail.

15. Crabbe, John., Belknap, John; and Buck, Kari: "*Science, Genetic Animal Models of Alcohol and Drug Abuse,*" Vol. 264, 17 June 1994, page 1717.

16. SCIENCE, op. cit.

17. *Alcoholics Anonymous* (affectionately known as the "Big Book" by AA members), author anonymous, AA World Services, NY, 1976. ISBN# 0-916856-00-3, pages 58-59.

18. Vaillant, George E., *The Natural History of Alcoholism*, Cambridge, 1983, pages 310-311. See also *The Natural History of Alcoholism Revisited*, Cambridge, 1995.

19. Ibid, page 311.

20. Literally, the Latin means "prior to the facts." The method of science must always be *a posteriori*, or after the fact.

21. In more cases depression pre-exists in alcoholics, but rarely is the etiology of the alcoholism rooted in it. Most often depression is a symtom of alcoholism.

22. Interestingly enough, on the last page of *Listening with the Third Ear*, Theodor Reik quotes Sigmund Freud himself as saying "I am not a Freudian."

23. Leven, Jerome *Treatment of Alcoholism and Other Addictions: A Self-Psychology Approach*, Northvale, 1991, page 71.

24. *Dynamic Approaches to the Care and Treatment of Alcoholism*, edited by Bear and Zinberg, NY, 1981, chapter by Vaillant, "*Dangers of Psychotherapy in the Treatment of Alcoholism.*"

25. *The Act of Surrender in the Therapeutic Process*, Harry M. Tiebout, NY, old and undated but available through Hazelden, Center City, MN.

26. Viking Press, NY, 1963.

27. *Civilization and Its Discontents*, London, 1930, as noted page 497 of Menninger's *Vital Balance*.

28. This is not to imply that addicts and alcoholics never lie; in fact they lie a lot, but the point is they truly believe they are neither "alcoholic" nor "addicted."

29. Op. cit., page 6.

30. *I'll Quit Tomorrow*, NY, 1973, page 28.

31. Op cit, page 51.

32. Ibid., page 49.

33. John 1:14, 17.

34. Form critics, those who have made a thorough study of the Bible similar to the studies literary form critics have applied to Shakespeare, dispute that John wrote this gospel.

35. John 8.

36. Luke 7:36-47.

37. *New Being*, NY, 1955, page 13.

38. In their defense I have to say they have reasons for this. Emotional overinvolvement with patients can lead to bad therapy, sexual involvement and lawsuits. It is dangerous, whereas underinvolvement may be useless. A therapeutic balance is called for, yet difficult to sustain.

39. Matthew 26:69-75, Mark 14: 69-72, Luke 22:58-62.

40. Matthew 25:31ff.

41. Matthew 6:19-21.

42. Matthew 7:1-2.

43. Matthew 5:44.

44. *Big Book*, page 96.

45. *The AA Way of Life*, NY, 1967, page 217. See also *Twelve Steps and Twelve Traditions*, NY, 1953, page 55.

46. Ibid., page 55.

47. Op. cit., pages 10-11.

48. Contrary to this obvious fact, some well-meaning physicians treat existential anxiety with tranquilizers. Existential anxiety doesn't need to be treated; it needs to be coped with, faced, lived with.

49. "No Nirvana Without Samsara," *Pilgrimage*, Vol. 6, No. 2, Summer 1978.

50. The New Being, NY, 1955, pages 34-42.

51. The Churches and the Third Reich, Vol. One: 1918-1934, by Klaus Scholder, translated by John Bowden, Philadelphia, 1977. See also *The Chief Rabbi, the Pope and the Holocaust*, Robert Weisbord & Wallace Sillanpoa, New Brusnwick, 1992.

52. Op. cit., page 38.

Chapter IV
Surrender

Surrender is all around us if we will only dare to see it. It is scary and painful. It is also promising. A caterpillar spins a cocoon and crawls inside. It is dark, like a tomb. Eventually the insect will fly away, a magnificent butterfly.

A bulb is buried in the ground. It will not sprout until next spring. A seed is planted amidst dirt and manure. When its time has come it will break through the soil and blossom.

It happens to humankind also. As Jesus of Nazareth said,[1] "Whosoever will save his life will lose it, but whosoever will lose his life...will save it."

A similar spiritual resonance rings in the AA words "Let go and let God" and Jesus' words "The last shall be first."

This classic spirituality of surrender is at least as old as the Hebrew prophets; yet it was always a bit out of fashion, taken seriously by a few poets, saints and prophets. To their number has been added in our day recovering addicts, alcoholics and some of their family members.

Classic spirituality has always been dwarfed by the much larger and more powerful secular forces of greed and power, older than the biblical "gather into barns" mindset and as contemporary as today's Dow-Jones average. This "gather into barns"[2] faith of secularity insists on arranging things and people, stepping on others to get ahead, hoping against hope that to be secure is to be alive. Its adherents are betting the first shall be first. They always seem a little anxious.

The secular mind does not comprehend the spiritual mind. Nicodemus had a secular mind.[3] When Jesus told him the spiritual path was rebirth, that he must be born all over again, Nicodemus responded like a modern biblical literalist wanting to know how he could "enter the second time into his mother's womb."

There come those times when we are powerless to change things. Often at such times our only hope comes through acceptance: that to be alive is to be insecure, that sometimes we must be last, that dying to self is best, that we must let go of something or someone precious.

Long before undertaker death there are little deaths in life, insults to our bodies as we age, insults to our souls if we become addicted.

We can accept what we cannot change, or we can refuse, trying courageously — foolishly — to change something beyond our capacity to change it. We lack the wisdom to know the difference between what to accept and what to change.

As the Preacher[4] reminds us, there is a time for everything, "a time to plant and a time to pluck up...a time to weep and a time to laugh...a time to be born and a time to die."

There is a time to surrender and a time to win.

The greatest of all spiritual paradoxes is when the time comes to win by surrender. We can save our life only by losing it.

A friend described to me his first night at Alcoholics Anonymous. He was sweating, shaking and wanting a drink more than anything. He looked at the old man sitting next to him and said, "God, I want a drink!" The old man looked back at him, put his arm around his shoulder and said, "Son, there comes a time when you just have to sit still and hurt."

There is a time to sit still and hurt. There is a time to surrender.

Jesus had to do it, in the garden, the night he was betrayed.[5] Alcoholics do it. Members of Al-Anon do it. Cocaine addicts do it.

We admitted we were powerless over alcohol—that our lives had become unmanageable (Step 1 of Alcoholics Anonymous). Surrender!

We admitted we were powerless over our addiction—that our lives had become unmanageable (Step 1 of Narcotics Anonymous). Surrender!

Surrender will work! But you say, "You mean just give up and keep on drinking?" Not really, although that may be a necessary way station for some on their way to recovery, because surrender means to stop fighting. Willpower is surrendered, in fact the surrender of the will is the essence of surrender! From the moment of this final surrender and the concomitant cry for help, the drinker may have to continue drinking until help arrives.

As the Big Book puts it, "I knew from that moment that I had an alcoholic mind. I saw that will power and self-knowledge would not help."[6] Or, "The fact is that most alcoholics, for reasons yet obscure, have lost the power of choice in drink. Our so-called will power becomes practically nonexistent." [7]

Until the fight is over there lurks in the addict the notion that somehow, some way, some day, she/he can return to the battlefield and fight again. Addicts want to believe "I can enjoy a drink (a joint, a snort, a hit) or two and then stop."

The fight is not over until the day of surrender. Yet surrender seems cowardly, unpatriotic and even un-American. It seems unmanly.

I sit amidst the Shenandoah Valley as I write this. I am surrounded by some magnificent ghosts. The grave of Thomas Jefferson is forty miles to the east. A little further northeast is George Washington's Mount Vernon. Thirty-eight miles south of me is the grave of Robert E. Lee.

Although he was on the wrong side of history, Lee is considered by many Virginians to be as quintessentially American as his compatriots buried nearby. His father, Light Horse Harry Lee, was a friend of and fought with George Washington. Lee married Mary Custis, the grandaughter of Martha Washington.

He was brave, bright and the only cadet ever to complete West Point without a single demerit. To say he was superb at military command understates his talent. He owned no slaves and was opposed to slavery. He was the only commander given the choice of which army — North or South — he would lead in the Civil War.

I believe Robert E. Lee personifies American manhood at its best in surrender. When the time came he surrendered like the officer and gentleman he was.

After his victory at Chancellorsville in 1863 Lee seemed invincible. But defeat at Vicksburg and Gettysburg followed soon after. It took until Eastertide 1865 to whip him, however.

Stonewall Jackson and Jeb Stuart were dead and Lee's forces were "scarecrow thin and scarecrow ragged."[8] He was outnumbered four to one and his troops were largely "old men and shoeless boys, as young as fourteen."[9] Even these men were melting away from him.

Little Phil Sheridan had torched the entire Shenandoah, and Tecumseh Sherman had destroyed half of Georgia. Richmond had fallen.

Grant had Lee cornered near Appamattox. As one soldier put it, "He couldn't go forward; he couldn't go backward and he couldn't go sideways."[10]

He held a council of war. Some urged surrender; others said fight on. General Alexander wanted Lee's army to "be like rabbits or partridges in the bushes, and they could not scatter to follow us."[11] Shelby Foote describes that scene:[12]

> Lee heard the young brigadier out, then replied in measured tones to his plan. "We must consider its effect on the country as a whole," he told him. "Already it is demoralized by the four years of war. If I took your advice,

then men would be without rations and under no control of officers. They would be compelled to rob and steal in order to live. They would become mere bands of marauders, and the enemy's cavalry would pursue them and overrun many sections they may never have occasion to visit. We would bring on a state of affairs it would take the country years to recover from. And as for myself, you young fellows might go bushwhacking, but the only dignified course for me would be to go to General Grant and surrender myself and take the consequences of my acts." Alexander was silenced, then and down the years. "*I had not a single word to say in reply,*" he wrote long afterwards. "*He had answered my suggestion from a plane so far above it that I was ashamed of having made it.*"

Others were in denial. A woman in Richmond said, "We tried to comfort ourselves by saying in low tones...that the capital was only moved...that General Lee would make a stand and repulse the daring enemy, and that yet we could win the battle and the day."[13]

Still others remain in denial today, rationalizing the surrender away, projecting the blame onto the "Yankees" and riding about with confederate-flag bumpers stickers.

No so General Lee! The awesome commander knew when it was time to surrender. He said, "There is nothing left me to do but go and see General Grant and I would rather die a thousand deaths."[14]

* * *

As Tiebout put it, "Surrender means cessation of fight and cessation of fight seems logically to be followed by internal peace and quiet...the whole feeling tone switches from negative to positive."

Surrender is no mere submission. Tiebout continues, "In submission, an individual accepts reality consciously but not unconsciously. He accepts as a practical fact that he cannot at that moment lick reality, but lurking in his unconscious is the feeling 'there'll come a day'...submission is a superficial yielding, tension continues." With authentic surrender the unconscious is actively involved; "there is no residual battle, and relaxation with freedom from strain and conflict ensues...the greater the relaxation, the greater the acceptance of reality."[15]

* * *

The United States could not begin its recovery until Lee surrendered, as he was painfully aware. As the Civil War historians say, before that war when we spoke of ourselves we said "The United States are," after it we said "The United States is." From a scorched, broken and bankrupt South, from a country grieving its dead both North and South, with so many men trying to adjust to life without their painfully amputated arms and legs, we recovered. That recovery is impressive.

* * *

When the intervention on an alcoholic or addict is done correctly, the clan has gathered, along with the alcoholic's employer, family and friends. With support and empathy and in non-judgmental terms, Fred is told concrete truth he has managed to avoid. If he can hear enough of that truth to knife through some of his invincible ignorance, he "would rather die a thousand deaths" than admit it. He is tempted t o run away like "like rabbits or partridges in the bushes." A day after surrender there may come ideas rushing from the basement of his mind: he was "rushed into seeking help" and he's "no worse than anybody else." In such cases his counselors and family must be as merciless and relentless as Grant pursuing Lee.

Can Fred surrender? Some "Freds" do; others are unable. In their invincible ignorance they fight to the death.

Insane belief in willpower dies a hard death. The temptation to "run like rabbits" and fight another day is often more compelling.

* * *

The Twelve Steps[16] have many roots, but their taproot is in William James.[17] In substance those roots translate as follows for alcoholics:

1. Alcohol defeats the person. All human resources such as willpower, intelligence, education and determination have failed.

2. The person accepts this defeat. Attempts at denial, explanation and justification fall away. The person feels both helpless and hopeless.

3. The person cries out for help. This cry may or may not be in spiritual terms.

4. The help arrives with directions and instructions. The subject follows the directions even though they make little sense to him at the time.

The subject trusts the helper.

5. By now a dramatic change in mood has occured, from, "What's the big deal, I'm not hurting anybody but myself" to "Oh, my God! I had no idea I was hurting so many of you."[18]

Like General Lee, Fred surrenders his sword, relinquishes command and does as he is told.

If the family and treatment team are as gracious as General Grant, great care is taken to preserve Fred's dignity.

Some crack cocaine addicts surrender; others fight on, robbing and stealing to support their habit. Some alcoholics surrender to treatment and AA, others drink, on defiantly "brawling" and "bushwhacking" their way through life.

Invincible Ignorance destroys addicts who are unable to surrender.

They must surrender to survive. It is time to think of others, their family, those they love. As Lee said, "It would take the country years to recover."

When one is trained to recognize it, surrender is virtually palpable. (It is true there are those con artists, those "professional patients" who have been in treatment so often they can fake it.) Fred's whole countenance changes as he passes from compliance (with defiance lurking in the basement) to surrender.

There is resolve in his voice and a bounce in his step. There is no hesitation as he says, "My name is Fred and I'm an alcoholic." His statement has gusto. It is becoming a part of his very identity. This acceptance has a fresh and precious but naive quality to it. Fred will tell you he is *never* going to drink again. He is in the time of the "pink cloud."

As surrender deepens, there is another emotional change. Fred becomes more sober in the ancient sense of that word, more in touch with reality, more "down to earth." He has found some humility. His feet are on the ground. He is more savvy and more wary. If you ask if his drinking days are over he will say something like, "I hope so. I know I have another drunk in me but I'm afraid I don' t have another sobering up in me. All I have is today." Then he adds that he is going to a meeting later this afternoon.

His mind is made up and he wants to keep it that way. He knows as long as he attends meetings and talks to his sponsor, he *can* keep his mind made up.

* * *

For some, surrender comes quickly and is very dramatic. For others it is more incremental and protracted. Much of what happens is deep inside the head and heart. It is private.

First Lady Betty Ford has been gracious enough to share her experience of surrender from alcoholism and tranquilizer addiction.[19]

> Now those doctors wanted me to admit that I was an alcoholic. They wanted me to make a public statement about it. I refused. "I don't want to embarrass my husband," I said. "You're trying to hide behind your husband," Captain Pursch said. "Why don't you ask him if it would embarrass him if you say you're an alcoholic?" I started to cry, and Jerry took my hand. "There will be no embarrassment to me. You go ahead and say what should be said." With that, the crying got worse. When Jerry took me back to my room, I was still sobbing so hard I couldn't get my breath. My nose and ears were closed off, everything was closed off, my head felt like a balloon. I was gasping, my mouth wide open, sure my air was going to be cut off. I hope I never have to cry like that again. It was scary, but once it was over, I felt great relief.

* * *

Sooner or later surrender becomes grief — deep, seemingly bottomless grief. It was so for Betty Ford. And so it is for every alcoholic and addict trying to get through the passageways.

Ethyl has been left behind. She will be sorely missed.

It can also be the beginning of the end of isolation, depression and humiliation.

As Ethyl is left behind, new friends begin to gather about the alcoholic who has connected with other recovering persons. Fred is now asking help on a daily basis, from his counselor, his sponsor and from his Higher Power.

There is a shaft of light ahead in the passageway. It is hopeful, a moment of calm. In this barest glimpse of serenity it occurs to him to appreciate the "here and now" or, in Twelve-Step language, "one day at a time."

The beginnings of gratitude are evident and for a few minutes Fred is slightly less willful and self-centered. He can taste humility for the first time and he likes the taste. His humility is no groveling, simpering kind of self-deprecation. You can see it in the way he walks with his feet on the ground, on the same level as everyone else. Very shortly he will miss Ethyl but right now his defenses are down.

Tiebout further describes surrender:

> The forces of defiance and grandiosity actually cease effectively to function....the individual is wide open to reality; he can listen and learn without conflict and fighting back. He is receptive to life, not antagonistic. He senses a feeling of relatedness and at-oneness...of inner peace and serenity...the individual no longer fights life, but accepts it....reality (is) a place where one can live and function as a person acknowledging one's responsibilities... (making) reality more livable for oneself and others. There is no sense of "must", neither is there any sense of fatalism....The state of surrender is really positive and creative.

Although counselors cannot make surrender happen, they can learn to recognize it when it does happen and they can learn to get that surrendered patient quickly into the company of other recovering persons. That is the only reliable way I know to preserve this change of attitude from negative to positive.

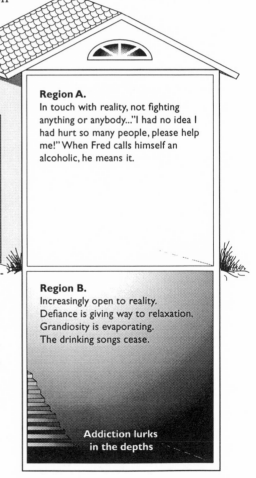

Region A.
In touch with reality, not fighting anything or anybody..."I had no idea I had hurt so many people, please help me!" When Fred calls himself an alcoholic, he means it.

Region B.
Increasingly open to reality. Defiance is giving way to relaxation. Grandiosity is evaporating. The drinking songs cease.

Addiction lurks in the depths

Figure 3. SURRENDER
A construct picture of the mind.

ENDNOTES

1. Luke 9:24.

2. Matthew 6:26.

3. John 3:1-13.

4. Ecclesiastes 3.

5. Mark 14:36, Matthew 26:42, Luke 22:42.

6. page 42.

7. Ibid., page 24.

8. *The Civil War, A Narrative*, Vol. 3, Shelby Foote, Vintage Books, NY, 1986, page 941.

9. *The Civil War, An Illustrated History*, Geoffrey Ward, Ric Burns and Ken Burns, Alfred A Knopf, NY, 1990, page 365.

10. Ibid., page 378.

11. Op. cit., Foote, page 942.

12. Ibid., emphasis mine.

13. Op. cit., Ward, page 370.

14. Foote, op. cit., page 941.

15. Tiebout, op. cit., page 8.

16. See Appendix I for a listing of the Twelve Steps.

17. *The Varieties of Religious Experience*, by William James, NY, 1917. from the Gifford Lectures delivered at Edinburgh in 1901-1902. It was this work Bill Wilson was given to read by Ebby in Towns Hospital in New York in 1935 after Bill's "white light" spiritual experience. Equally miraculous is the fact his befogged brain, still in acute withdrawal from ethanol, could make sense of such difficult reading.

18. One of the best descriptions ever of this is in Chapter 5 of Johnson's *I'll Quit Tomorrow*, op. cit.

19. *The Times of My Life*, by Betty Ford, Harper & Row, NY, 1978, pages 284-285.

Chapter V
The Donner Pass

Surrender has brought an emotional shift within Fred, from depression to a bouyant mood with a bounce in his step. The fighting has stopped. Tension is replaced by relaxation, what Betty Ford termed "great relief."

However, surrender must deepen if it is to be sustained. Denial still lurks in the basement corners and shadows.

Life seems hopeful again, but that hope must be balanced with humility. It may seem callous to counsel humility for one so overburdened with dis-esteem and shame. Yet the way through this passageway is neither by pride nor by unwarranted self-confidence. By its very nature pride is the threshold to arrogance. "I *did* it" too easily becomes "*I* did it." The hope comes from the community of other recovering persons who surround Fred in the treatment center and in AA.

Without hope there seems no reason to press on; yet false hope in a bankrupt self will result in disaster.

Alcoholics and addicts in early recovery are *starving* for self-confidence and self-respect, but if Fred forgets that his strength and hope come from the support of those around him he will be easily seduced into belief in himself alone. "Himself" has been getting Fred drunk and keeping him drunk for years. By Twelve-Step definition, such confidence in himself is insane!

This misplaced belief in self-confidence plagues addicts, their families and, unfortunately, even some psychotherapists. Belief in self, or self-confidence, and belief in a Higher Power are polar opposites. As long as the addict still professes belief in himself, surrender has not occured.

"Step 2. Came to believe that a Power greater than ourselves could restore us to sanity."

Cocaine addicts come for treatment, they tell their stories, hear lectures and watch videos, have therapy sessions, go to group, "take" Step One, confess their relapses; many go right back out and use. A few begin recovery and never look back.

Failure to negotiate the passageway of the Second Step destroys many addicts and alcoholics. The Second Step is the first major encounter with spirituality. It bewilders and frightens many addicts.

The old English word "pass" is rooted in the older French and the ancient Latin. In its most primitive form it simply meant a "step," a "pace." To "pace off" means to "step off" marching. A pass leads to a passageway, the route to somewhere one wants to be. An impasse, then, is a blocked passageway. You can't get through.

Since the mid-twentieth century, drunks, junkies, potheads and crack smokers have been stepping through Twelve Step passageways to sobriety and serenity.

Some heroin addicts recover in Narcotics Anonymous. Others almost do, but use again. Some finally make it. Others never bother.

Some alcoholics go to Alcoholics Anonymous and make it for a while "two stepping." They work only the first and the last steps, trying to hopscotch around the others. They admit they are powerless and march straight off to help others. They are ready to "carry the message," but they don't yet understand the message.

They stumble, they slide and they "slip." They are trapped in the passageway. They fall. They get hurt. They never make it through. The crack addicts smoke crack again, to their own bewilderment. Their families are frightened and angry.

Some can't find the entrance. Others find an opening, then darkness. Many are haunted by old demons lingering along the way. Some see light momentarily, like a flash of lightning on a hot summer night. Then it is dark again, and they give up the journey. A dimly lit barroom or crack house seems warmer and more friendly.

They cannot make it through the impasse. They cannot make it through the passageway of the Second Step.

* * *

In 1846 the Reed and Donner families left Illinois for California. By November they had reached the place we now call the Donner Pass in the Sierra Nevada Mountains. The snow, ice, freezing winds, and eventually starvation blocked their passageway. Of the original 87, only 47 made it through to California. The other 40 perished. Several were eaten by their starving companions. Only half could step through the passageway.

Is the Donner Pass too harsh, too abrasive a metaphor for the Twelve Steps? I think not! Is there an alternative route, another way through? A "solution-focused" shortcut?   A few other passes have been tried. For most travelers they are even more dangerous.[1]

Forty-seven out of the original 87 of the Donner Party is a 54 per cent success rate. Substance abuse recovery is even more hazardous. Most of us know of an alcoholic suicide or death by a crack overdose. Many have read about adolescent drug dealers shot down in the street. Less newsworthy are the alcoholics with "wet" brains or addicts with "fried" brains. None of them made it through the passageway.

Others, however, continue to make it through.

* * *

There *is* a way through, but the going is tough. As they say in Narcotics Anonymous, it's simple but it's hard as hell.

There are many perils in the passageway, in several regions; each has its own traps.

THE INSANITY PERILS

Alcoholics and drug addicts have suffered remorse, criticism, guilt, shame, embarrassment and humiliation. To admit, "My name is Fred and I'm an alcoholic" seems one injury too many. Addicts are asked to suffer two more insults: 1.) To admit that their lives are unmanageable, and 2.) To ask to be "restored to sanity." They must continue to shed their invincible ignorance.

First the shock of the insult — the implication of insanity — must set in. It must be accepted by the patient.[2] Once this reality has a firm grasp on Fred-the-patient it helps him understand more nearly what is meant by "insanity."

As mentioned above, it does not mean the crazy behavior of drunkenness.

It is insane to keep trying the same old solution and expecting different results. Swearing off alcohol hasn't worked yet. Fred told the judge he would never get another DUI.[3] He went through ASAP.[4] A few months later he got still another DUI!

You wanted to believe your son when he promised he wouldn't smoke pot any more, but he did — again and again.

Attempts at self-control failed last time. Willpower did not work the time before. It is insane to believe the same old solution will work *next* time.

Suppose you saw me beside the road trying to fix my flat tire. You see me jack up the car about halfway and the jack collapses. I try again, and again and again. Each time the jack collapses. You start to laugh. Each time I get a little angrier yet still more determined, hurling profanity at the "damned" jack, tire and car. A crowd has now gathered to watch me. I still haven't tried anything different, just old-fashioned main strength and awkwardness. You reckon this next attempt is my sixteenth try! Would you not think me a bit insane? Or at least invincibly ignorant about changing a flat tire?

Drunks and junkies are not lying when they promise to "cut back," "swear off" or vow to "go on the wagon." They mean it. And if you believe they can, that is *your* insanity. The diseased will has become impotent to control the body's ingestion of alcohol or drugs.

The Big Book[5] describes Second Step insanity this way:

> Our behavior is as absurd and incomprehensible with respect to the first drink as that of an individual with a passion, say, for jay-walking. He gets a thrill out of skipping in front of fast-moving vehicles. He enjoys himself for a few years in spite of friendly warnings. Up to this point you would label him as a foolish chap having queer ideas of fun. Luck then deserts him and he is slightly injured several times in succession. You would expect him, if he were normal, to cut it out. Presently he is hit again and this time has a fractured skull. Within a week after leaving the hospital a fast-moving trolley car breaks his arm. He tells you he has decided to stop jay-walking for good, but in a few weeks he breaks both legs.
>
> On through the years this conduct continues, accompanied by his continual promises to be careful or to keep off the streets altogether. Finally, he can no longer work, his wife gets a divorce and he is held up to ridicule. He tries every known means to get the jay-walking idea out of his head. He shuts himself up in an asylum, hoping to mend his ways. But the day he comes out he races in front of a fire engine, which breaks his back.
>
> You may think our illustration is too ridiculous. But is it? We, who have been through the wringer, have to admit if we substituted alcoholism for jay-walking, the illustration would fit us exactly. However intelligent

we may have been in other respects, where alcoholism has been involved, *we have been strangely insane.* [Emphasis mine] It's strong language—but isn't it true?

The insult of being labeled insane is perilous, especially to an ashamed person, a frightened person, a person in deep dis-esteem. It takes real humility to accept this Second Step, but not to accept it is to return to the humiliation of more drunkenness. Even for newcomers who meet regularly with those recovering people who have accepted the Second Step, it is difficult and takes time. Yet there is obviously hope in this route; those who have taken it are so alive!

PERILS ABOUT GOD

Drunks and junkies may be insane, but most aren't stupid. They know a "Power Greater Than Ourselves" is our soft-pedaling euphemism for God. They have been arrested, then prayed over in jail by preachers. Some have at least a slightly self-righteous spouse, active in church, appearing innocent and long-suffering before the world. A few were sexually molested as youngsters by priests. Others have been moralized over by prohibitionist Sunday School teachers. Still others are gangsta-rap-loving, poverty-born adolescents who live in the streets, mistrusting all authority, holding the "Just Say No" world in utter contempt and suspicious of the gods of the Establishment.

If you're out of jail now but your name is in the paper, and if you are broke, lawyerless and having trouble remembering what happened the night they caught you (you were in a blackout, and can't remember what happened), you probably dread clergy types coming to "help" you. Your defenses are up and you may be very reluctant to talk about things spiritual.

Or, you're a crack addict. Up until a year ago you could claim, "If I am hurting anyone it's only myself." But now you're out of cocaine and you've already sold your mother's jewelry and written a half-dozen hot checks.

*   *   *

There is still another problem simultaneously hounding Fred, a cloud of free-floating anxiety, a sense of impending doom left over from his drinking days. It haunts him when he is alone, awakens him in the night. Let us turn to that before returning to his simultaneous struggle with the Higher Power.

ANXIETY PERILS

We are all restless. Another term for that restlessness is existential anxiety, mentioned above.

Fourteen centuries ago St. Augustine said, "Our souls are restless." Everyone has a restless soul, addicts and alcoholics even more so. They drank to quiet the anxiety. They smoked pot to sedate the restlessness. Now the sedation has worn off and the restlessness has rebounded with a vengeance!

Existential anxiety is not pathological anxiety; it is not a form of mental illness. *Everyone* has it. Tranquilizers are only palliatives. At worst, tranquilizers are what AA refers to as "eating your booze." NA members see the tranquilizer as just another drug from which they are trying to recover, alongside pot, heroin and cocaine.

It is normal anxiety, also called everyday anxiety, basic anxiety, fundamental anxiety or ontological anxiety. It is existential because it cannot be eliminated; it goes with the territory of being alive. It is restlessness.

Existential anxiety is sometimes subtle, often outside our awareness. It seems just to float about us.

Will Herberg, a Jewish theologian, lectured at length about it.[6] For Paul Tillich it was a favored theme.[7]

Types of Existential Anxiety are:

1. The Responsible Character of Existence. To be responsible is to be anxious. Anyone in a leadership position understands this. The administrator is responsible for what the agency does, yet the administrator has only partial control over what employees do. Administrators are paid well for bearing anxiety. Yet even the most humble employees understand this if they have children. We have only partial control over our children, but we are accountable for much of what they do. To be a parent is to be anxious.

2. The insatiable character of existence. Tillich said,[8] "Man [is] always dissatisfied with what is given him." We never get enough. When we get what we think we want, the shine soon wears off the new cars and new lovers. In the song, "Just Keep on Dancing," Peggy Lee used to sing, "Is this all there is?" King Solomon of the Bible had everything: wealth, many wives, concubines, much power and a marvelous palace. Yet he cried, "Vanity of vanities, all is vanity!"

3. Everyday Guilt. We wish each other a "good day" knowing full well how much guilt we can accumulate before bedtime. Sheldon Kopp said, "Our best way may not turn out to be good enough. Still it will have to do." [9] So he recommended, "Learn to forgive yourself, again and again and again and again..."[10] To be guilty is to be anxious. Who will find me out and criticize me? Tillich distinguished between the anxiety of existential guilt, which he said was relative, and the anxiety of condemnation in life, which he called absolute.[11]

4. The amphibious character. In a sense we are amphibious creatures. We belong in two worlds. Tillich called them the historical and the eternal.[12] On the one hand, we are animals who have emerged from the primordial ooze, as our body odors and sexual glands never let us forget. On the other hand, we belong somehow to another order, a "little lower than the angels." We are spiritual beings who pray and contemplate life after death. We concern ourselves about morality and ethics. Our bodies make demands. Our souls issue other orders. We are caught in the middle. Mark Twain said we are the only animals that blush.

5. The forlorn and estranged character. Everyone — no matter how famous — feels cut off and estranged at times. Poets understand. A. E. Housman referred to himself as "a stranger and afraid in a world I never made."[13] Tillich drew important distinctions between loneliness and solitude.[14] He said "Loneliness can be conquered only by those who can bear solitude." It produced painful anxiety even for Jesus: "He went up into the hills to pray. When evening came he was there alone."[15]

In spite of mental health, good nurture, financial security and sound adjustments, life is an anxious affair. Life is difficult, every day!

So what is the point? Am I saying existential anxiety causes addiction and alcoholism? No! But I am saying what is known by nearly everybody who has been under anesthesia, taken a tranquilizer, had a cocktail or smoked a joint. Sedation removes anxiety. Daily drinking, drugging is a little daily vacation from anxiety.

Drunks and junkies have been escaping existential anxiety for years. They have much to learn about coping. They are spiritually disabled. They can't do what others have been doing for years. They tried to get through life without paying full dues.

For addicts and alcoholics trying to quit, the problem is compounded by the indescribable anxiety of withdrawal: acute and post-acute. Acute withdrawal anxiety is pathological, but fortunately it usually lasts only a few days! Some addicts have tremors and shakes. Others have hallucinations. Convulsions may seize and terrify anyone in acute withdrawal.

Often a return to sedation seems the only hope. For the relief of the moment, no price seems too high to pay.

Post-acute withdrawal can last for a year and include vivid dreams, nightmares, insomnia, a heightened sense of smell and taste, temporary sexual impotence in men, anhedonia (joylessness), itching, twitching in the legs, occasional dizziness, hair loss, growth of new hair, muscle spasms, weight gain, weight loss, and other idiosyncratic reactions as the nervous system readjusts itself to sobriety.

Existential anxiety rebounds with a vengeance. Twelve Step group members empathize, "Yeah, reality sucks, doesn't it?"

Existential anxiety lurks about the passageway of the Second Step. It leaps unexpectedly from behind the rocks in the passageway.

The proper "therapy"[16] for existential anxiety is immersion in a strong spiritual community of friends. Although psychiatrists and clinical psychologists are trained to treat pathological anxiety, they have little or no training with existential anxiety. Spirituality is the treatment of choice.

Alcoholics and addicts in early withdrawal are confused and standing as judges against themselves, condemning themselves deeper and deeper into self-rejection and despair. They have lost their spiritual moorings and many contemplate suicide. They despair of finding any sense of destiny, of a place that is theirs in this world.

For most — if not all — of us, a sense of destiny is a spiritual yearning. Tillich believed we all yearn to belong to God, even those of us who deny God. Tillich said, "Man tries to escape God and hates Him, because he cannot escape Him. The protest against God, the will that there be no God, and the flight into atheism are all genuine elements of profound...faith."[17] The psalmist (Psalm 139) also contends this is true. We cannot escape God. There is nowhere to go where God isn't!

With spirituality comes a reliance on a "god" of some description. Hence the "god peril."

THE GOD PERIL

Such a problem is this that the Big Book devotes the entire Fourth Chapter (entitled "We Agnostics") to the subject. For example:

> ...Many times we talk to a new man and watch his
> hope rise as we discuss his alcoholic problems and explain
> our fellowship. But his face falls when we speak of spiri-

tual matters, especially when we mention God, for we have re-opened a subject which our man thought he had neatly evaded or entirely ignored.

We know how he feels. We have shared his honest doubt and prejudice. Some of us have been violently anti-religious. To others, the word "God" brought up a particular idea of Him with which someone had tried to impress them during childhood.[18]

Alcoholics Anonymous and Narcotics Anonymous redefine the word "spiritual," insisting their groups are not religious. They are pro-spirituality, insisting it is a *sine qua non* of recovery. "Religion" is suspect to many members of AA and NA. The Preamble is read at the beginning of each AA meeting. It says, "AA is not involved with any sect, denomination... organization ...neither endorses nor opposes any causes." When a deity is mentioned it is always qualified as "a Power greater than ourselves" or "God as we understand Him." Tradition Two insists, "For our group purpose there is but one ultimate authority — a loving God as he may express Himself in our group conscience. Our leaders are but trusted servants; they do not govern."[19]

Fortunately, there are the old-timers around who remember their own past despondency. They tell the newcomer, "I used to think I did not believe in God. Then I came to understand that the truth of the matter was that I just did not think God believed in me. It was you people [in AA] who have made me see through your lives that God does, after all, believe in me."

This doesn't make the newcomers instant converts! But it may open their minds so they can listen. They may "take the cotton out of their ears and put it in their mouths."

First the newcomer must realize who God isn't! This often comes as a shock.

Ernest Kurtz entitled his history of Alcoholics Anonymous *Not God*.[20] The epigraph is,[21] "First of all we had to quit playing God." He says this is "the message of the A.A. program."

The old-timers tell the new person, "All you need to know about God is that you're not Him." They explain that as they told lies, rearranged the facts of their drinking to suit themselves, wreaked hurricane-force havoc, broke laws and generally became a law unto themselves, they were acting as if they thought they were all-powerful. Not accepting the world as it is (the one God created), they tried re-creating a world of their own design.

They might even say to the "baby" recovering drunk, "It's obvious you've been believing in your own willpower. Believing in yourself ain't working! Why don't you try getting out of yourself? Consider something greater than yourself for a change. That might help."

The "God problem" has two traps in which those on Twelve Step journeys through the passageways get caught: A. Does God Exist? and, B. Projectional.

A. DOES GOD EXIST?

Faith, "the substance of things hoped for, the evidence of things not seen"[22] is by its nature ambiguous.   Contrary to popular belief, even the Bible is sympathetic toward doubters. Mark describes a believing doubter saying to Jesus, "Lord, I believe; help thou my unbelief."[23] Jesus himself was tolerant of doubters. When Thomas doubted the resurrection of Jesus, his doubt was accepted with empathy.[24]

In the *Dynamics of Faith*, Paul Tillich[25] describes faith and doubt as inseparably linked. It is impossible to have faith without genuine doubts. He explains:

> Faith is uncertain...This element of uncertainty in faith cannot be removed, it must be accepted. And the element in faith which accepts this is courage....The risk to faith...is indeed the greatest risk man can run. For if it proves to be a failure, the meaning of one's life breaks down; one surrenders oneself...to something which is not worth it.

Religious faith, standing-in-church-and-saying-the-creed faith, can be shallow. Recovering faith must be existential, or it won't work. (One theologian defined existential faith as "red hot right now" faith.) Faith carries an existential risk, can cause great anxiety and is somewhat like gambling. Patients in substance abuse treatment sometimes understand it as:

WHEELBARROW FAITH

You and a companion are standing in the street in Manhattan looking up at the World Trade Center towers. Way, way up there someone has stretched a tightrope from the top of one tower across to the other. You can't actually see the rope, but you can see a man walking across it. You can just make out that he is pushing a wheelbarrow.

Your companion wants to wager and says he'll bet you fifty dollars "that fool" won't make it. You continue to watch the tightrope walker and decide he knows exactly what he's doing. You call his bet.

Is your belief a form of faith? Yes, but it's not yet existential faith.

Your companion then says, "If you're so sure, I'll bet you a thousand dollars you won't go up there and ride across sitting in the wheelbarrow." Riding across in the wheelbarrow is existential faith.

Believing a Power greater than yourself can keep you clean and sober is existential faith. Everything rides on it.

Faith is difficult. No matter how clever we are, the ambiguity never evaporates. Who has not prayed, all the while wondering if anyone was listening? As you ride across the tightrope in the wheelbarrow you have to believe in the man pushing from behind. You are afraid to look down. Faith always includes doubt.

Some say they "hear" an answer to their prayers. Bible stories describe God "answering" prayers.

The Bible doesn't say Moses figured out a message in his mind so that it seemed as if this were God's reply to his prayers. It never says it was a little like a daydream with slightly less authority than a sound-asleep dream. It says the "voice" was "heard"; the "Word" of God was spoken.

"Ezekiel saw the wheel," says the Bible. And yet, if I told you — as we both look skyward — about seeing the wheel, what might you ask yourself? If you are a substance abuse counselor, you might wonder if I were a danger to myself or others. You might wonder if I were on LSD or mushrooms. You might even consider a commitment to a mental institution for me. When Ezekiel does it, we call it faith.

Logical arguments seldom convince anyone to believe. Yet counselors often try them. It is well to discuss the arguments and the fallacies.

Since before the time of Socrates to the high Middle Ages, philosophers and theologians have used one version or another of five classical arguments. The five classical arguments are based on: 1.) authority, 2.) cosmology, 3.) teleology, 4.) ontology or 5.) morality.

I. Authority: Biblical infallibility, papal infallibility, ecclesiastical infallibility, clerical (bishops, priests, preachers) authority.

Consistently in his research, replicated throughout the western world, Stanley Milgram found that two out of three people will believe any established authority. Milgram established that authority takes on a "suprahuman character.... Few people have the resources needed to resist authority."[26]

One-third of the population is not so easily convinced. They are skeptical and think for themselves. For sceptics and scientists, facts outweigh authority. Mistrust of authority is common among junkies and drunks. You can feel a rebellious ambience in most any AA meeting. Arguments for God based on authority tend to backfire.

II. Cosmology: The argument is from the Greek word *cosmos*. It assumes everything has a cause. It says the cause of the cosmos was God.

It makes sense, since almost everything we know about had a cause. Yet science cannot allow such an assumption. Maybe the universe just always *was*.

The problem is the little girl in the second row. After the preacher tells the children that God made the world, she asks, "Yes, but who made God?" The preacher tells her that "God is eternal. There never was a time when God was not." The little girl says, "Yes, sir." And keeps her doubt to herself. Twenty-five years later, when she is a full-blown alcoholic, she is even more sceptical.

III. Teleology, from the Greek *telos* meaning "end," argues that we are obviously headed somewhere with a purpose. Teleology talks of our destiny and God's purpose for us. It says things like "God is not finished with me yet."

It is comforting to believe that someone is in charge of this world who knows what he or she is doing. We want to believe this.

The problem is that for some life seems random, as if no one is in charge. Quantum mechanics suggests our existence is a crap shoot.

The existentialist Jean-Paul Sartre insisted that life is absurd, a bad joke, and the joke is on us.

Who can say? If you are a cocaine addict in withdrawal, suffering anhedonia and depression, feeling worthless, you can reach Sartre's conclusion easily.

IV. Ontology (from the Greek *ontos*, which means being) was argued by Anselm of Canterbury in the 12th century and Paul Tillich in the 20th. It is a circular argument really, saying that since folk have an idea of God there must be a God. Even "pagans" and aborigines conceptualize a god.

The problem is that the idea of the Easter Bunny is also widespread in America. Ideas do not make things true.

V. The moral argument says that morality is universal. All humans seem to have some sense of right and wrong. It argues that this morality was put there by God.

Yet Freud and many others argue that morality came from our parents and those around us, not from God.

Besides, not all cultures have the same morality. Bigamy, abortion, cannibalism or incest might be acceptable in one culture and not in another. Did God teach one morality to one people and another morality to another?

EVIL

But the strongest argument *against* the existence of a god is the problem of evil. Evil is sometimes obviously "natural": earthquakes, floods, plagues, droughts and cancer. Why does one child inherit the cystic fibrosis gene and not another? How could a good God allow such evil? As Archibald MacLeish put it in *J.B.*, "Either God is God and He is not good, or, God is good and he is not God." If God isn't responsible for the evil, who is? Is God so helpless he cannot prevent some (d)evil from contaminating his creation?

Genocide, cystic fibrosis, childhood malignancy and violence done to infants challenge pious platitudes. What can one say to parents after a child's funeral that is comforting yet has integrity? That Jesus took that child "home to be with him?" That is not much help when the parents return to the baby's bedroom and empty crib! How can a good God allow such suffering? Or, how can a strong God stand by helplessly as other forces do their evil to children?

Unresolved struggles with the problem of evil probably result in more honest atheism than any other cause.

The classical arguments never convince one who does not want to believe.

In addition to the philosophical questions, we all have our own personal issues with God. An alcoholic in early recovery may be a bit like a pouting teenager. Fifteen-year-old George is so angry at his father that he walks right past him in the living room, ignoring his existence. The pouting adult crack addict denies the existence of his "father" in the heavens. Both are in pain, feeling they cannot get their needs met. George wants to "teach the old man a lesson."[27]

Those in early recovery are in intense pain and shame. It is all they can do to cope. They hide their self-contempt, their remorse, shame, despair, depression, anhedonia and guilt as best they can. Free-floating anxiety chases them.

One way to organize such a cacophony of negative emotions is through bitterness and anger. But once they have been galvanized into such resentment there are only two alternatives: 1. turn it inward, on themselves, at which point, it becomes depression — and very possibly suicide! 2. Turn it outward onto counselors, wives, bosses, children or God Himself. The passive way to hate someone is to deny his or her existence.

A decision to believe existentially comes from somewhere beyond reason. It is not irrational, but neither is it contrary to reason. Existential belief is trans-rational. It reaches across reason to grasp us. It is not hostile to logic. It is simply *beyond* logic. Something deep within us is grasped by something powerful outside of us.

This is a little like the way some people decide to marry. They look at all the reasons on both sides. They sleep on it. Then something in their "heart" tells them.

This is also how people surrender their fight against addiction. Something very, very different reaches out to them.

B. PROJECTIONAL

At the beginning of the century Sigmund Freud pointed out how we transfer or project our attitudes, fears, prejudices and admiration onto gods we create for ourselves in the heavens.[28] We do not have to agree with Freud's atheistic conclusions to learn from him. Believers can realize how much our own faith has been prejudiced by our own life experiences. An example of what I mean is the case of Roberta Bondi.

Although neither an alcoholic nor an addict, Roberta Bondi, a professor at The Candler School of Theology, Emory University, describes from her own experience the hidden power of such childhood attitudes projected onto the heavens. Her experience with the "god problem" is so similar to what many recovering persons experience that I choose it as a model.

An Oxford graduate, Professor Bondi is a rare and articulate believer. She is open, honest and highly self-aware. Her childhood and early adult understandings of God were theologically pathological.[29] They made her ill, spiritually ill.

She was reared in a world of revival meetings and the preaching and teaching of a Baptist church in Union County, Kentucky. She believed herself "rotten to the core." She thought God was so enraged with her he had sentenced her to be executed. As a child she had learned the Bible stories of Abraham and Isaac. She knew God had ordered Abraham to kill his beloved son, Isaac, as a sacrifice. God had done this just to test

Abraham, to make sure Abraham didn't love his son more than God! The Old Testament God was "jealous."

She had been offered an escape. As if God were some kind of plea-bargaining lawyer, He would settle for the "shameful murder of Jesus in her place." This may have been temporary relief to her, but it hardly inspired confidence in God. It would not be long in a little girl's imagination before the god became a bloodthirsty, out-of-control member of a lynch mob, "out to get somebody!"

Young Roberta had a childhood dream in which she was "strapped into a dentist's chair in a darkened church basement, my eyes fixed feverishly on a neon cross on the wall while the devil danced around me, dental instruments in hand."

In spite of her theological sophistication and training at Oxford she had a similar, more horrible dream as an adult.[30]

> Then, on the eighth night I had a terrifying dream. I dreamed I was with Richard [her husband] in my great-aunt Blacky's farmhouse on the hill outside Morganfield, Kentucky. It was the middle of a good-smelling early summer day with the insects humming and the hassock fan whirring on the front porch. Sunlight poured through the kitchen into the back hall where I stood, but I was in darkness. I was sobbing and wringing my hands outside her green-tiled bathroom. In the bathroom Richard was kneeling in the bathtub, his neck held over the drain by a powerful looking, dark-haired man with a huge knife. I knew he had come to kill me. "Don't hurt her," Richard was saying. "Take me; just don't hurt her. Take me."
>
> In my dream I was dying with grief. I wanted to shout, "No, no; I'm here. Leave Richard alone," but I couldn't make any sound. As I watched in horror, the killer slit Richard's throat and red blood flowed all over the green tiles.

This is the terror a sophisticated theological mind can feel towards God.

Most alcoholics and addicts do not have the advantage of an Oxford theological education. Some have heard the words of I Corinthians 6:10 from childhood, that no "drunkard shall inherit the kingdom of God."

They get into substance abuse treatment. They enter the perilous passageway, and encounter the statement "Came to believe that a Power greater than ourselves could restore us to sanity." Some are paralyzed with fear on the spot, trapped in the passageway. Others turn and run back toward the entrance. Others try to make it through without a Higher Power and are caught up in their drug again. Many die in the passageway.

Logical arguments do not have the power to counter experience. This does not mean there is no hope, nor does it mean God, or the Higher Power, is inaccessible. It means reason will not get us there. The hope is in the power that has changed the lives of so many drunks and junkies who have gone before. The hope is in following their path, in going the way they went, in dreaming what they dreamed and practicing what they practiced.

In the language spoken by Tillich (as quoted above) it requires a "power that shakes us and turns us and transforms and heals us." In the language of William James and Carl Gustav Jung it is a conversion experience. In the language of AA with the religion removed, it is simply, "Having had a spiritual awakening as a result of these steps..."

ENDNOTES

1. Psychoanalysis, Ego Psychology, Drinkwatchers, Moderation Management, Transactional Analysis, Gestalt, Rational Recovery and behavior modification procedures are some of the other therapies tried. Other have attempted treatment with other substances: Antabuse, Methadone and Naltrexone. Success by way of these other routes is so unusual that most substance abuse counselors do not recommend them.

2. Literally a "patient" is a sufferer, from the same Greek root that we get pathology, pathetic and pathos. A patient in a hospital suffers. For the victims of addiction (which includes other family members) the word "patient" is far more appropriate and descriptive than the innocuous word "client."

3. "DUI" means a charge of driving under the influence of alcohol or drugs; in many states the initials DWI refer to driving while under the influence.

4. An Alcohol Safety Action Program, which is a set of educational classes and/or therapy groups for those convicted of DWI or DUI.

5. Op. cit., pages 37-38.

6. For this paradigm I am indebted to an undated, unpublished paper of the late Will Herberg of Drew University.

7. Tillich never got far from writing about it; it is in most everything he wrote. His most systematic treatment of it is in *The Courage To Be*, New Haven, Yale University Press, 1952. His graduate student, Rollo May, was also eloquent on the subject. See *The Meaning of Anxiety*, Pocket Books, NY, 1950 and *The Courage To Create*, W.W. Norton, NY, 1975.

8. *The Shaking of the Foundations*, NY, 1948, page 52.

9. From "No Nirvana Without Samsara: An Assortment of Life's Ironies," *Pilgrimage, The Journal of Pastoral Psychotherapy*, Vol. 6, No. 2, Summer, 1978.

10. *If You Meet the Buddha on the Road, Kill Him!*, Science and Behavior Books, Ben Lommond, 1972, page 166.

11. *The Courage To Be*, op. cit., pages 51-53.

12. *The Shaking of the Foundations*, op. cit., page 23.

13. *Last Poems, XII*.

14. *The Eternal Now*, NY, 1963, pages 15-25.

15. Ibid., page 23.

16. Ironically, the Greek root for therapy is sometimes translated "to worship" in the New Testament. In the Greek-speaking world, including the early Christian Church, a "therapist" was an attendant. The therapist attended either to suffering patients or to the cultic priest at the temple. The temple was closely associated with healing. In the classical world, therapeutic treatment and spirituality were two pieces of one whole cloth.

17. *The Shaking of the Foundations*, op. cit., page 45.

18. Op. cit., page 45.

19. *Twelve Steps and Twelve Traditions*, Anonymous, AA World Services, NY, 1952, page 132.

20. Hazelden, Center City, MN, 1979.

21. Ibid., page vii.

22. Hebrews 11:1 (KJV) emphasis mine.

23. Mark 9:24 (KJV).

24. John 20:24-29 (KJV).

25. *Dynamics of Faith*, Harper Torchbacks, NY, 195b7, pages 16-22.

26. *Obedience to Authority*, Stanley Milgram, Harper & Row, NY, 1974.

27. I am indebted here to Bishop Fitzsimmons Allison, author of *Guilt, Anger and God*, Seabury Press, NY, 1972, pages 81-85.

28. *Moses and Monotheism* as cited in Freud: Dictionary of Psychoanalysis, ed. Nandor Fodor and Frank Gaynor, Wisdom Library, NY, 1958, page 34.

29. *Memories of God*, Abingdon Press, Nashville, 1995.

30. Ibid., pages 112-113.

Chapter VI
The Way Is Trans-rational

So, if reason and logic are less than convincing, how can patients "come to believe"?[1] Once in a meeting of Alcoholics Anonymous I heard Ken O. put it this way:

> I cannot control my brain. This is not an intellectual program. AA is not a mind-control exercise, but a spiritual program. I cannot by naked will or thought control stay away from the first drink. Neither naked will nor thought control will keep me sober. My safety net is here, a spiritual safety net. It's not my thinking at all. It's not in my brain.

In other words, the spiritual power transcends the rational mind. It is trans-rational.

Professor Bondi (see Chapter 5) had a corrective spiritual reaction.[2] It took place over a period of months and years. Her change began at Oxford while studying a sixth-century Monophysite bishop who believed in a "generous and gentle God." She turned next to the ultra-orthodox, fourth-century Athanasius, who convinced her of a kind Father God who cared enough to mount a rescue for her. He "came among us" to bring healing and love. She realized, "For some inexplicable reason, God actually liked us."

As she purused the works of other early Christian monks she could hardly believe what she was reading. Instead of self-serving she found altruism in God; instead of meanness she found kindness; instead of deception she found honesty. What she was reading challenged her "older images of God." It meant a major rearrangement of her feelings and attitudes of "not just my relationship with God, but the very shape of my relationship with my husband, my father, my mother and myself."[3]

Through her relationship with her new husband, who "not only loved me; he liked me" and her new role as mother she found new ears through which to hear a God of love.

Instead of a cruel and sadistic father-god of the skies, she saw Jesus through the eyes of a mother:[4]

> I experienced myself standing in the yellow dust of Golgotha at the very foot of the cross...I stood by Jesus as his mother. Under the blazing sun, as close as I was allowed to be, I stood there feeling the heat radiating from the legs of this man who was my child, and my heart was breaking. All I could remember was the baby he had been, his sweetness, his arms around my neck, his nursing mouth.

Professor Bondi had found her own way to make spiritual sense out of her life, to find *God as she understood Him.*

Like everyone in such a passageway, she experienced profound confusion before knowing clarity. The fear died as the love was born and nurtured in her.

Such spiritual healing has been found throughout the centuries. It arrived for Isaiah the Prophet in the Temple at Jerusalem in the eighth century B.C.,[5] for Saul of Tarsus on the Damascus Road in the first century of the Christian era,[6] for Augustine of Hippo on the veranda of a villa in Milan in the early fifth century,[7] for Martin Luther in the tower of his monastery in the early sixteenth century and for John Wesley at Aldersgate in the eighteenth century. It happened for the anonymous author of the *Cloud of Unknowing* in fourteenth-century England.

While these experiences are similar, they all differ. One would be foolish to try to replicate Bondi's experience, or Isaiah's. Each person has his or her own relationship with the Higher Power. Each is unique. This uniqueness is part of the special intimacy with God as we understand Him.

When the help arrives, it must be accepted. This may be the hardest part of all. So often, the prescription is refused by the patient. Such a case was Naaman's.[8] He was a leper. He was also a commander of the army of the King of Syria. He came to Elisha asking for healing. Elisha told him to wash in the Jordan River seven times and he would be healed.

Instead of taking the prescription, he objected vigorously. He preferred to wash in the Abana and Pharpar rivers instead. They were cleaner. He criticized Elisha: "I thought he would at least have come out and stood, and invoked the Lord his God by name, waved his hand over the place and so rid me of the disease." He was not ready to surrender his care to another.

Fortunately for Naaman, he later heeded the counsel and washed in the Jordan. He was healed.

Like Naaman, alcoholics are given a healing prescription which they often resist. If they can willingly wash in Alcoholics Anonymous instead of the River Jordan, and do this seven times a week — week in and week out — they will experience a miracle themselves. But they must "stay until the miracle happens."

This passage is often as perilous for addicts as it was for Naaman. Naaman saw the Jordan River and its people as undesirable. Before their first few meetings, alcoholics often think of AA and its people as undesirable. The same is true of addicts before they go to NA. They are afraid "someone" will see them there among the undesirables.

And yet, many of us believe alcoholics and addicts are on a spiritual quest, and have been on one, if only *in potentia*, for a long time. Many drunks have sat, listening to music, alone, holding the bottle and reading the label. They read "neutral grain spirits" and they wonder...

They almost cradle the bottle. It has such worth! It is adored, worth-shipped.

They also realize that when — or if — they go to AA, the bottle must be left behind.

Can they find the courage to make it through this passageway in Alcoholics Anonymous? If they can and if they keep on "washing" each day, they may feel the tug of spirituality. There is an attraction in this strange community. At first it is hard to see because the spirituality is casual and fleeting. It is easier to see in some meetings than in others. One needs to "keep coming back."

Although they may not even be able to admit it to themselves, alcoholics are afraid of saying good-bye to Ethyl. She has rescued them from boredom, anxiety and isolation-in-a-crowd. She has saved them from painful emotions: guilt, shame, depression, and despair. She has put them to sleep when no one else could. She has done this in such profoundly somatic ways, in ways well-nigh sensual. From the head on down the back of the neck and beyond, as the muscles relax and the nerves loosen up, the whole body remembers Ethyl.

Cocaine addicts insist even more strongly how sensual, how somatic is the memory.

Ethyl, Mary Jane or Coke may have become religious for them, although they would be the last to admit it. Religion comes from the Latin verb *religare*, meaning to bind, to hold together. Our ligaments hold us together. Ligaments literally hold your leg together at the knee.

Think of *re-ligion* as your figurative "re-ligament," meaning whatever holds you together.

As Howard Clinebell said,[9] "One will not fully understand alcohol as a problem until one sees it as a solution." No matter how destructive the rest of us perceive alcohol to be, the alcoholic believes in it as the solution to his problems.

Ether, opium, Fentanyl and other kinds of anesthesia have "saved" us from the pain of surgery much as Joshua of old "saved" his compatriots in battle from their enemies. The notion of Joshua as savior is lost in the mists of primitive religious times. Joshua, who "fit the battle of Jericho," is the ancient form of the name Jesus.

When addicts and alcoholics first enter the spiritual domain of AA or NA, they are ambivalent about what they want to happen there for them. They are attracted to the new life, yet pulled back toward the old familiar life. The desire to quit hurting is balanced against a desire to keep on drinking and/or drugging.

THE MIRACLE

One side of the ambivalence shows a growing positive identification with these attractive recovering alcoholics.[10] These people have finished grieving the loss of Ethyl. They have gusto and they do not feel deprived. They do not regret the past, because their lives are now of such value as to convince them that the price they have paid in reaching this state of life was worth it.[11]

The newcomer is able to put these old-timers to the test of phoniness. They pass the test. The newcomer tries to fake his serenity, but is told to be on guard. The ambivalence will return. The newly recovering person will soon want both the joys of sobriety and the remembered euphoria of turning back to the bottle. The hell of withdrawal is soon forgotten.

Life with alcohol seems unthinkable. They'll say, "I don't even want a drink anymore. I don't even think about it." Yet, another part of them, outside of awareness, thinks a life without booze inconceivable.

The experienced recovering people understand these ambivalent feelings and encourage newcomers to explore them with the group's support. Slowly, they learn how to "think through a drink," to visualize its consequences before they drink!

Newly recovering alcoholics are more dependent on the group's support than they realize; they need other recovering people. Again and again they learn how to live another day without having to drink.

At this stage, this "cunning, baffling and powerful" disease is faced in a realistic way. After hearing it over and again, the newcomer begins to understand that "*We* can do what *I* cannot do alone."

Hope emerges. Newly recovering persons often say something like, "Finally I found some hope! You people have shown me a way I could live without booze and yet live with myself. I never would have believed it."

The newcomer needs these people; they have great worth-ship to him. When Fred finally got into AA, he realized he needed to do what the others were doing. Simultaneously he experienced his past beckoning to him.

Since his drinking was largely solitary, something he did "on his own," Fred was tempted to try to get sober on his own. At such times he needed to be a part of the AA team, the "we" who keeps doing what "I" cannot do!

An even worse peril lurks for many. For those tormented like Roberta, terrified of the god-of-her-childhood, there is a full-grown dragon lurking ahead, the "god crisis."

Meetings of Alcoholics Anonymous and Narcotics Anonymous begin with prayer. In this newfound, friendly and hopeful place some newcomers hear an alien language. They do not want to renounce these folk and this new hope. They may look forward to the meetings and the human warmth, but complain of the "god bit."

The unselfish human support seems indispensible. Yet they fear that sometime they may be asked to return to the god of their fathers, the god of the Green Tiled Bathroom.

A contest is in progress, a contest between gods. It is not unlike an Old Testament god contest presided over by Elijah who was predecessor to Elisha.

Elijah knew his people would not forsake an idol as long as it produced results. In Elijah's time the idol was Baal; today the idol is obviously Ethyl, Mary Jane or Crack.

Elijah called for a demonstration. Four hundred and fifty prophets of Baal called all morning on the name of Baal to light the fires of sacrifice. Elijah taunted them that Baal must be asleep or out of town. It became clear that Baal could not light their fires. For dramatic effect, Elijah had them drench the sacrifice in much water. In the evening, when Yahweh's time of sacrifice came and they called upon Him, not only did He instantly light the fire, but it worked so well that everything nearby was devoured in flames.

There was no doubt in anyone's mind that this new God-as-we-understand-Him (in this case Yahweh) could light the necessary fires.

A Green Tiled Bathroom god cannot light the fires of sobriety. Such a god simply cannot deliver the experience, hope and strength of recovery. If the newly recovering person can hang around long enough, and not leave "before the miracle happens," in all probability he will find — or be found by — a fresh, new and exciting god he uniquely understands. This new god can light the fire, the hope of sobriety.

Some travelers are burdened with a Green-Tiled-Bathroom type of god well along their passageway. Functionally they rely on the group as their Higher Power. They may be unable to pray and still retain their integrity.

The group is patient with them. There are those present who were once too cynical to pray themselves. They understand. They know the new folk are trying. They are doing the best they can with brains that until recently have been heavily marinated in alcohol. They are trying to discover their way to "understand," to believe, to commit themselves. The AA program is not there to take away their minds, but to take away the ravages of their addiction. They are given guidance along with increasing freedom to develop their own interpretations.

The older members are powerless over the new person's spiritual awakenings, and they know it. They let him be as he is, yet they do not abandon him.

All newcomers are struggling to relinquish control, to allow themselves to be helped. The old-timers realize they cannot control the newcomers, and so they remind each other, "We can only carry the message; we cannot carry the alcoholic" through the passageway.

ENDNOTES

1. Some patients will claim belief in a Higher Power to please their counselor.

2. A neologism. From categories of depth psychology Franz Alexander coined the term "corrective emotional reaction." It means a deep, unconscious correction of an older negative emotional experience abreacted into the present. It is relived, so to speak. The meaning of the phenomenon is changed from negative to positive, from fear and hatred to love, from disease to health. Hence, a corrective spiritual reaction means much the same, but it is engendered by spiritual rather than merely psychological forces.

3. Op. cit.

4. Ibid., pages 139-140.

5.   See Isaiah 6:1-8.

6.   Acts 9.

7.   See the *Confessions of St. Augustine*.

8.   II Kings 5:1-15.

9.   *Understanding and Counseling the Alcoholic*, Abingdon, Nashville, 1956, page 57.

10. AA describes itself as a program of "attraction rather than promotion" in its Eleventh Tradition.

11. This is not to imply they are indifferent to the hurt they have caused others. A significant part or their recovery is making amends to others as they are able.

Chapter VII
On Through the Passageway

Anyone in a dangerous passageway has the urge to move too quickly through the scary places. Like corporate executives or politicians in trouble, addicts in early recovery speak of "putting all that behind me," as if it were virtuous to skip quickly over serious problems and ignore them.

Their mentors counsel patience. The enterprise of drinking and drugging absorbed a lot of time. This recovery is going to take time too, at least as much time as drinking took!

Fred used to begin his day by coming to, as opposed to waking up. He tried to confabulate his blackout period, the time he could not remember. He had a painful dialogue with himself about last night's drinking, and decided not to drink tonight. Later, in the early afternoon, he reconsidered this as his body withdrew from the lingering sedative effects of the ethanol. He changed his mind. Then he purchased his whisky and thought of how to explain his decision to drink to June. Next he drank for several hours. Then he passed out and began to sleep it off.

This all took a lot of time, at least an eight-to-ten hour exercise. When he finally stopped drinking, he was like a man who had lost his job. He had too much time on his hands.

If he is not going to an AA meeting every night, it is especially difficult. Sitting around trying not to drink is a little bit like trying not to think of a hippopotamus. Try it for a minute. Just sit still and *don't* think of a hippopotamus!

However, if he comes home, has a shower and a change of clothes, has an early supper with his family, then goes out to pick someone up and take them to an AA meeting, then goes out for the "meeting after the meeting" for coffee, then comes home, he has restructured his time significantly. If he can do this seven nights a week, he's getting 24-hour immunity from his desire to drink. He has also altered not only his drinking time but his "thinking of drinking" time.

Certain things of value in this life take time to accomplish, and recovery is one of them. Think two to five years in the passageway. Old habits take time to change, even in the company of those who can show you how to change them.

* * *

As alcoholism progresses, it becomes chronically and insidiously antisocial. Fred needed more alcohol than his friends did, so he found new friends to drink with, often his inferiors. This eventually progressed to lone drinking. Just "me and Ethyl; I don't need nobody else, to hell with them," he said to himself.

With early sobriety he thought he needed his old friends, those with whom he drank. He was right about needing companionship, but his old drinking buddies? To be with old friends who get together to drink while he explains how he is "on the wagon" is not only difficult but dangerous. It is a slippery place. He is placing himself in a situation where he has to be antisocial in a new way. The drinking group socializes with drink. He keeps ordering iced tea as they order another round of beers.

Even if they do not try to tempt him to drink; even if they protect him ("Charlie wouldn't allow me to drink"), he is still at a disadvantage. They sit there enjoying their buzz while watching him abstain. Even assuming he is not eaten up with secret envy, he will inevitably experience it as condescension.

The fastest route to new and interesting friends is again the AA group. Here Fred can find those who are like him, who have similar needs and interests.

* * *

His culture is against him. If Fred is the John Wayne type he sees his two-fisted hero shoot the bad guys, then sit with his buddies and do some two-fisted drinking. The United States Congress gave Wayne a medal for playing this role over and over.

Madison Avenue advertising professionals understand this very well. They can package booze in Wall Street success or any way you like. A scotch whisky ad once had a young black executive in a three-piece Brooks Brothers suit flying first class. You got the picture; he was important. It said, "Socked in over Boston, socked in over New York and socked in over Washington; time to launch another Cutty Sark."

If you are a woman who fears her waning sexual appeal, advertisers have it packaged for you in sultry velvet or sexy shades of satin. The psychology of this is highly sophisticated and slightly sacramental. It reminds me of *Alice in Wonderland*. Like Alice, women find a bottle with a "drink me" label on it which promises instant change. In Lewis Carroll's tale, Alice would experience dramatic, instant change in size. The whiskey ads promise that women who take this and drink it will become softer, sexier and more appealing. What an effective wonderland fantasy it is.

The best way to buck a culture is to find a home in a counterculture. AA and NA are countercultural in the sense that they vigorously support a life free of mood-altering chemicals amidst a wider culture fascinated with pills and potions to make you sleep, stop your aches and pains, quiet your anxiety, even make your hair grow!

Step Three. Made a decision to turn our will and our lives over to the care of God *as we understood Him*.

Although he covers it well, underneath Fred's defensive facade hides his deep dis-esteem. In his damnation to isolation Fred thought he saw himself accurately, as ashamed, guilty and damned to a mighty thirst. He found such a description of himself in the Big Book:

> Selfishness — self-centeredness! That, we think, is the root of our troubles. [We are] Driven by a hundred forms of fear, self-delusion, self-seeking and self-pity...our troubles...are basically of our own making. They arise out of ourselves, and the alcoholic is the extreme example of self-will run riot, though he usually doesn't think so. Above everything, we alcoholics must be rid of this selfishness.[1]

Although "self-will run riot" accurately describes Fred's recent lifestyle, it is only a limited, truncated picture of Fred. But for now, newly in the state of surrender, it is all Fred can see. It is frightening, perilously so.

There is another part of Fred still dormant, outside his awareness. As God sees us, all of us, there is more good in the worst of us and more bad in the best of us than we ourselves can see. Fred still confuses his *known* self with his *total* self. Fred is soon to correct his spiritual misperception of himself.

He hears others say "God is not finished with me yet" and he wonders.

Assuming there is a God who created Fred and who sustains Fred, God sees what Fred cannot. As an ancient prayer has it, for God "all hearts are open, all desires are known." From Him "no secrets are hid."[2]

For now Fred bridles at what seems to him a voyeuristic God, this God who sees inside his bedroom twenty-four hours a day. He sees only the scathing judgment and misses the compassion, the nurturing, healing care about to bring gracious change in him.

Nikos Kazantzakis put it this way: "God leans over and blows on the worms...the worms must become butterflies. We are become butterflies, not simply immortal worms." Fred sees accurately what a worm he is; he has not a clue that a butterfly is hidden inside him, waiting to be born. His God has "better things" in store for him "than he can even desire or pray for."[3]

This is one of the darkest times of passage. Something must die in Fred. Fred is like the worm going into its cocoon, dark, constricted, coffinlike. He cannot see the future. All seems hopeless. His companions in AA keep telling him, "It gets better." He tells them, "Damn, I'm tired of hearing that!" But he keeps coming back.

Those around him in Alcoholics Anonymous understand what C.S. Lewis meant when he said, "The hardness of God is kinder than the softness of men." As I said earlier, the program is simple but hard as hell. Those who have gone before know what a crucible experience is the surrender to spiritual awakening. They guide the newcomer as gently as they can along the rocky passage. They would also agree with John Donne that "God's hand is in this." Of that they are quite sure!

For now Fred is not asked to actually live by the will of this "god." He is asked to think about it, consider it and, when ready, to make a decision about it.

Now is not the time for Fred to go looking for God. Now is the hour to be still and to let God approach him, in the companionship, in "the Fellowship." God-with-skin-on-Him[4] must do for now. This is frightening enough! As C. G. Jung put it:[5]

> Simple things are always the most difficult. In actual life it requires the greatest discipline to be simple, and the acceptance of oneself is the essence of the moral problem and the epitome of a whole outlook upon life. That I feed the hungry, that I forgive an insult, that I love my enemy...all these are undoubtedly great virtues....But what if I should discover that the least among them all, the poorest of all the beggars, the most impudent of all the offenders, the very enemy himself — that these are within me, and that I myself stand in need of my own kindness, that I myself am the enemy who must be loved — what then? As a rule the...attitude is reversed; there is no longer any question of love or long-suffering; we say to the brother within us "Revenge!" and condemn and rage against ourselves. We hide it from the world; we refuse to admit ever

having met this least among the lowly in ourselves. Had it been God himself who drew near to us in this despicable form, we would have denied him a thousand times before a single cock had crowed.

* * *

Fred's cocoon is frightening. His only support is the bunch of butterflies flying around him. Can he allow himself to be grasped and changed? He need only "make a decision" for today. That is risky enough.

* * *

FORGIVENESS

Addicts and alcoholics need forgiveness just like everyone else, only more so.

On the other hand, they do not need to be excused. Being excused is quite different from being forgiven. If someone borrows your car, gets drunk and wrecks it, then hopes you'll say "That's OK, the insurance will pay," that's excusing him.

Forgiveness comes after he sees your pain, feels remorse and pays the damages. It does matter and you let him know it. You struggle to forgive him. It is not easy. It was a new car and you had carefully protected it from scratches and dents — until he wrecked it! Forgiveness is difficult for most of us. For many of us, it sometimes seems impossible.

Jesus of Nazareth was never facile with words of forgiveness. I suspect he understood how hard it is to forgive, but I also suspect he knew the brokenhearted plea in those who try to live without forgiveness. Interestingly enough, he never said the words "I forgive you." (Possibly he thought that came across as condescending.) What he said was "Your Father in Heaven forgives you," or "You are forgiven." I am not suggesting he thought forgiveness unimportant, quite the contrary! I think he realized how much power it took to forgive and how easy it was to mouth empty words of forgiveness, words which cheapen the reality of forgiveness.

Both the Twelve Step tradition and classical Christianity believe forgiveness must come from above.

By Twelve Step reckoning, forgiveness is the business of Step Five. Before that comes the hard, written homework of Step Four.

Step Four. Made a searching and fearless moral inventory of ourselves.

Although this step indicates it is to be taken fearlessly, I have yet to meet anyone who was not afraid of it. For Fred, to take it fearlessly means he goes ahead even though he is afraid. (For me this means a courageous moral inventory.)

This step needs to be written: "We set them on paper."[6] Like any serious writing, some is done every day. The secret is in the rewriting as much as in the writing. Like shaking down the burning logs in the fireplace with the poker and watching the sparks fly, one idea sparks another, and more blaze up.

These papers must be locked away between writing sessions. They are for no one else's eyes.

Fred is nearing the end of his solitary times.

Just as important as the relief of shame and guilt is another purpose of this step. It is the beginning of the end of invincible ignorance. It is the morning star of the day when Fred can begin to see himself as God sees him.

Soon Fred begins to wonder who will be the other human being who will hear this step from him. Obviously this is a perilous time; fear of it has sent some back to the bottle. Yet many return to active addiction *because* they did not take this step. They continue in confusion, alternately judging themselves too leniently, then too harshly. For Fred the blindfold of invincible ignorance is about to be removed.

Step Five. Admitted to God, to ourselves, and to another human being the exact nature of our wrongs.

Making accurate judgments about someone's true guilt may be impossible. Jesus of Nazareth counseled against it.[7] Jesus understood that only God was intelligent, informed, kind, wise and fair enough to judge accurately.

Fred has defended himself so long — rationalized, projected, minimized and compared — that he has lost touch with his guilty self. It is time to sort out his conscience.

Why is God present? Because God is the only one smart enough. OK, if God is present, why does anyone else need to be there? Because without a witness, without someone to make an appointment to do it with, it either won't get done or won't get done properly. This step is too important to hop-scotch over. In another sense, the other human being represents God, some would say "God-with-skin-on." The other human being brings an objectivity which Fred alone can never bring to himself. Perhaps most people are more afraid of revealing themselves to another human than to God.

Finally the day had come. Fred looked his counselor, Mr. Babcock, in the eye, to see if he was shocked. What a relief he wasn't. But Fred needed to tell it all, so that after he left he would not wonder, "but what if I had explained that other part of it, what might he have thought then?" When he got to the part he had saved until near the end he was really afraid. He described how once, while drunk with a homosexual acquaintance, he tried to experience homosexual sex. He was so ashamed! Yet his counselor never blinked. And there was Oscar, his old faithful dog. Oscar had loved him so. But because Oscar was too much trouble during his drinking days, he had had the dog put down. He felt so guilty. He could still see that dog looking up at him, those eyes!

The forgiveness needs to be as total as is humanly possible. The shame must be cleared away, the garbage can of the soul cleaned and scoured.

With this cleansing often comes a new, drug-free euphoria, a real-life high, an honest high, followed by a new, more realistic self-perception. Fred has less guilt about many things, new guilt over new realizations. He now feels increased sensitivity and responsibility for his absences from his family when he had been passed out drunk. He knows he cannot change the past or undo what he has done, and he is not yet sure what he can do to make amends. Mr. Babcock counsels patience. That is further along in the journey, in Steps Eight and Nine. For now, the invincible ignorance is falling away.

Should the other person who hears this step be another AA member? Some say yes.[8] Others counsel the use of a professional: a physician, a psychiatrist, a psychologist, a counselor, a pastoral counselor, a minister or priest knowledgeable about addiction, someone who can professionally guarantee confidentiality. If professionals betray your confidence they can be held accountable before the law, but another AA member may appear to be more capable of empathy. One can find the best of both worlds by finding a substance-abuse counselor who is also an AA member.

Scary? You bet! But oh, so worth it!

This seems the place to distinguish between judgment and condemnation. What Fred does not need is condemnation, to be known fully and to be rejected. What he does need is judgment, honest, accurate judgment followed by profound forgiveness.

By accurate judgment I mean a slant on judgment most of us rarely see. I do not mean what we feel toward the person we see accused of a horrible crime on the televised news. Nor do I mean the district attorney's charges against this man, nor his attorney's defense. Neither do I mean the jury's verdict, nor the sentence imposed by the judge. By accurate judgment I mean something beyond all of these, something dwelling in another dimension. I mean the perception of guilt enjoyed only by an all-seeing, just, righteous and compassionate God. The kind of God described in the *Book of Common Prayer*,[9] a God "unto whom all hearts are open, all desires known and from whom no secrets are hid."

The more accurate the judgment, the more genuine the forgiveness. Genuine forgiveness is most often followed with a fresh desire to assume responsibilities.

G. A. Studdart-Kennedy articulates what I am trying to say: what true judgment is and how we fear it. He describes a World War I soldier on the battlefield dreaming of meeting his maker.[10]

> And then at last 'E said one word,
> 'E just said one word — "Well?"
> And I said in a funny voice,
> "Please can I go to 'Ell?"
> And 'E stood there and looked at me
> And 'E kind o' seemed to grow,
> Till 'E shone like the sun above my 'ead,
> And then 'E answered "No,
> You can't that 'Ell is for the blind,
> And not for those that see.
> You know that you 'ave earned it, lad
>
> So you must follow Me.
> Follow Me on by the paths o' pain,
> Seeking what you 'ave seen,
> Until at last you can build the 'Is'
> Wi' the brick o' the 'Might have been'."
> ....
> For I daren't face in the land of grace
> The sorrow of those eyes.
> There ain't no throne, and there ain't no books,

> It's 'Im you've got to see,
> It's 'Im, just 'Im, that is the Judge
> Of blokes like you and me.
> And, boys, I'd sooner frizzle up,
> I' the flames of a burning 'Ell
> Than stand and look into 'Is face
> And 'ear 'Is voice say — "Well?"

There is no condemnation here, although Fred feared it at first. Then, as he realized the condemnation was missing, he got more afraid, afraid of the truth. There was no punishment either, just judgment; honest, accurate judgment. Yes, he really has been a worm, a creepy, crawly, ugly worm. But there is so much more to Fred, parts of himself he has not even glimpsed, that only the God of his understanding can see. God is not finished with Fred yet.

Before Fred can soar as a butterfly he must live as a worm just a little longer.

On the way to becoming a butterfly, Fred will crawl out into the sunshine. As he crawls his legs will grow longer. Soon the crawl will become a walk. He will begin to walk among us.

Following this kind of "from whom no secrets are hid," God-viewed judgment there follows a genuine humility. But this is no whimpery, groveling obsequiousness. Humility, from the Latin *humus*, means "on the ground." Genuine humility is of the earth, its feet "on the ground." It is not "high," like a cocaine high soaring above the rest of us. Neither has it dug a hole and crawled down in it like a worm. Humility walks among us; its head is up and it looks us in the eye.

There is a rest stop at this bend in the passageway. Yes, there is still a long journey ahead, but now it is time to stop and breathe. But rest is not all this stop is about. It is time to begin to learn to live non-compulsively, to watch the lilies of the field grow and hear the birds sing. As one sponsor told his pigeon, "Go out in your back yard and hug a tree...learn to love it, enjoy it. It's time to learn to *be* and enjoy the rest of being. There is much more to life than doing, and it's time you began to realize this."

The following Sunday Fred stayed home while June went to church. He almost went with her, but decided at the last minute not to go. He could not explain it. He was just sure he was not yet ready for church. Yet almost simultaneously he felt a need to read or do something spiritual. He found a dusty old book of poems and sermons by John Donne. He got himself another cup of coffee and decided to take his time, maybe even enjoy meditating. He read for a while and nothing seemed to happen.

He got up to go for some more coffee but the taste in his mouth said no. He thought about television, but he did not want to see or hear any Sunday morning preaching. He sat down once again with John Donne. Then it happened.

Some words leaped off the page at him, words that Dean Donne had used to describe a sick and suffering man: *"For affliction is a treasure, and scarce any man has enough of it; no man hath affliction enough that is not matured and ripened by it and made fit for God in that affliction."* [11]

"Well, I'll be damned" said Fred aloud to himself. "No," said Fred, "I'll be quite un-damned!" It was just then he realized for the first time what his buddies in AA meant when they said they were "grateful" to be recovering alcoholics. They did not just mean they were glad they had recovered. They meant much more; much, much more! They were being "made fit for God!"

He thought of all the pain he had caused his family, his boss and himself. "Did I have to go through all of this, put them through all of this? Apparently the answer is yes." Then he remembered more words of Donne, in one those sonnets. He leafed quickly through his old college text book, and there they were. [12]

> Batter my heart, three-person'd God, for You
> As yet knock, breathe, shine, and seek to mend;
> That I may rise, and stand, o'erthrow me, and bend
> Your force, to break, blow, burn and make me new.

"Yes, yes, yes," he said. "Oh, it hurts, but it is happening to me! Today! It's been happening to me! I am sober by the grace of God and I understand exactly what that means!"

ENDNOTES

1. Big Book, op cit., page 62.
2. This prayer from the *Book of Common Prayer* opens the eucharistic rite and goes back to Alcuin of York in 8th century England.
3. *Book of Common Prayer*, prayer "For Those We Love."

4. A term not universal in the AA Fellowship, but understood widely in Shenandoah Valley AA. Since most of us have never seen God, the best we can do for now is to see God as He is manifest in another human being.

5. *Psychological Reflections*, page 214.

6. See description in Big Book, pages 64-71.

7. Matthew 7:1-5.

8. *The Twelve Steps and Twelve Traditions*, author anonymous, NY, 1952, Chapter 5.

9. Op. cit.

10. As quoted in *Fear, Love and Worship* by C. F. Allison, Greenwich, Seabury Press, 1962, pages 138-139.

11. Op. cit., from title page of this book, emphasis mine.

12. "Divine Poems" No. XIV., by John Donne from *The Poems of John Donne*, London, Oxford University Press, 1929, page 299.

Chapter VIII
York Minster and Louis Armstrong

There is embedded, I believe, down in the chassis of our existence, an elusive combination of faith and hope. It is beyond despair, but you can't get there except through the passageways of despair. Those willing to be open to it can find it, or allow themselves to be found by it.

Traditional psychotherapy can get you part of the way, but then that road comes to a dead end. The last part of the trip is through that nebulous, elusive route of spirituality. It is a journey without maps. (Even if earlier travelers gave you their maps, it would not help much.)

For an alcohol addict — or anyone else, for that matter — it begins in anxiety. Fred worried about his life, his lying, his deterioration. Then followed a hope, a false hope, a Pollyanna, Mary Poppins, everything-will-turn-out-OK-won't-it? hope. Fred convinced himself he could handle it next time, that it was not as bad as he had feared and that he was not really hurting anyone but himself.

Around the bend came the opposite, the bleakest, dark death. Things turned out worse than his darkest fears. Fred was overwhelmed.

This had to happen to Fred, as it has to so many others. Dr. William Silkworth, one of AA's earliest professional consultants, called it "deflation in depth." Again we must emphasize, this is the region of disillusionment (and possibly concomitant acceptance of reality) where suicide is most likely to occur. The irony is that the closer Fred gets to surrender, the closer he gets to possible suicide. Yet if professionals back off in fear, they will probably miss the moment of judgment and truth.

The result of backing off an intervention in fear may likely be what Karl Menninger called "chronic suicide...the phenomenon of self-destruction by irresistible addiction to repeated, excessive drinking."[1] This kind of "chronic suicide" is neither a pleasant nor a pretty way to die.

It is only beyond this place that a new faith emerges, a hope that is both real and strong, eyes wide open, in touch with reality.

I can only point in that direction. Descriptions must be metaphorical. Let me try.

I was up at York Minster one day, in the north of England. That medieval cathedral is of so many towering stones, each having absorbed centuries of spirituality. That afternoon they were aglow in stained glass light. I thought of the chants those stones had heard and the clouds of incense they had absorbed.

It was the burial day of my friend.

And larking they came, up out of that ancient crypt, those choirboys, poking one another and giggling until an older choir member hushed them. They fell into line.

The great organ keyed the tones for them as they began the *De Profundis*, Psalm 130, in Anglican chant crafted specially to electrify the meaning of Miles Coverdale's elegant 1535 translation. Suddenly those choirboys had a competence about them that was as relaxed as those stitched-over-once-again surplices they wore. And the evening shadows lengthened through the Gothic vaulting.

Slowly they processed around those giant pillars of stone and into the great chancel. Everyone could hear every syllable. As they cried out of the deep, "Lord, hear my voice," I was quite convinced that if they could not get God's attention, nothing could. When they sang Israel's name it had three distinct syllables. Anglican chant has a mystical quality I can only ask you to imagine. I cannot squeeze it into words.

De Profundis. Psalm cxxx.

Out of the deep have I called unto thee, O Lord; * Lord, hear my voice.

O let thine ears consider well * the voice of my complaint.

If thou, Lord, wilt be extreme to mark what is done amiss, * O Lord, who may abide it?

For there is mercy with thee; * therefore shalt thou be feared.

I look for the Lord; my soul doth wait for him; * in his word is my trust.

My soul fleeth before the morning watch; * I say, before the morning watch.

O Israel, trust in the Lord, for with the Lord there is mercy, * and with him is plenteous redemption.

And he shall redeem Israel * from all his sins.

* * *

I thought about old Jacob and how, after he had wrestled with God all night, his name was changed to Israel. And I remembered what Israel means: "I wrestle with God."

I wrestled.

Is anyone home up in heaven? Or are the skies just empty? Can anyone hear the voice of my complaint up there? Is God really "extreme to mark what is done amiss?" Is no one in charge up there? And what about my dead friend?

Or, worst of all, is it just one huge cosmic, bureaucratic indifference? Oh God, I hope not.

* * *

Over in New Orleans they are having a street funeral. The ones Louis Armstrong called the "old raggedy guys, the hustlers, the drunks, the good time Charleys" are there. They understand my questions. They understand hopelessness. The musicians understand, else they could not blow those blues through those horns so well.

They know about death and the rot of life. And, yeah! they've heard about next spring and how the flowers always come up again. But they also understand that next spring is still a long time away.

And besides, my friend and me too, we are more than just flowers.

At the New Orleans cemetery the body is lowered into the ground and the preacher says the words about ashes to ashes and dust to dust.

And then...ever so quietly, so as you do not notice it, the snare drummer takes the handkerchief from under the snare. He picks up the beat, so slightly at first. Then they begin to shuffle, not much more than a soft-shoe sort of shuffle at first. And they all begin to walk!

And then the saints begin to march. Then someone says "Hallelujah" and that catches on. They begin to strut! And dance.

* * *

Faith is at least as much something that jumps out and grabs us as it is something we decide to believe. My experience grasped me!

It embraced its own doubts, as I wondered if anyone upstairs was listening.

Faith has only partially to do with thinking. It is emotional, but not only emotional. It is something we decide to do, but is far more than a decision. It is more unconscious than conscious. And it is somehow more than the sum of all the above.

Nothing else dramatizes this for me as much as experiencing someone who has been in a coma for days receive Holy Communion. It is a not uncommon phenomenon. For days they have been unconscious, speaking not a word, yet when they receive the elements they open their mouths, then close them, while making the sign of the cross.

Faith is a "centered act" as Tillich said. And it is hard to locate its headquarters: the brain? the central nervous system? Where else? Tillich said it is ecstatic, meaning it stands outside any single function such as feeling, thinking or willing. Faith has a life of it own. Reducing it to one function — especially the thinking function of the brain — is to trivialize it into a caricature of itself.

It is that movement out of despair ("let thine ears consider well the voice of my complaint") blown so well through those horns. Then it shuffles along. Then it begins to walk! Finally it breaks out into such an ecstatic strut!

As the author of the Epistle to the Hebrews (11.1) put it, "Faith is the substance of things hoped for, the evidence of things not seen." It has more to do with hope than trying to believe 2 + 3 = 7.

Like wheelbarrow faith (see page 60) it is always high risk. It often emerges out of despair. Some have said it is not unlike betting in a poker game, waiting for the turn of the next card.

Genuine faith is humble and has none of that preacherly arrogance about it. It is never quite sure, certainly never cocksure. It carries a grace about it, a live-and-let-live grace, a there-but-for-the-grace-of-God-go-I quality.

As Bill W.'s *Twelve and Twelve²* reminds us, faith is difficult for those who think too much. Intellectuals are like Zorba the Greek's philosopher friend to whom Zorba said, "Philosophers are like grocers; they weigh everything." Yes, there is much good to being a critical thinker, and our faith must not ask us to commit intellectual suicide, but there is also a time when genuine skepticism passes beyond itself into cynical arrogance. It is the arrogance of a high-IQ'd brain.

This is especially true of addicts and alcoholics in post-acute withdrawal. You will remember this is the time of much anxiety, of despair and dis-esteem. Such people have so little self-respect left that they hold tightly to their arrogance; it seems all they have.

That faith is much more than a thinking thing is not new to members of AA and NA. Across the centuries many saints have tried to explain that faith is deeper, more profound and powerful than a thinking exercise. Such a one was the author of *The Cloud of Unknowing*.

Fourteenth-century England was a time of abundant spirituality. It was the time of Chaucer's *Canterbury Tales*, that delightful mixture of sexuality and spirituality. Chaucer understood completely how the two are inseparably entwined. His characters are as likely to copulate as pray. Pity it is that educators have sterilized schoolbook versions of Chaucer so that most students who read him to pass an exam miss the fun.

The fourteenth century was also a time of great English spiritual giants: Dame Julian of Norwich, Richard Rolle and Walter Hilton. And one more!

As if anticipating Alcoholics Anonymous's Tradition Twelve ("Anonymity is the spiritual foundation of all our traditions...") by six hundred years, he managed to retain his anonymity for spiritual reasons. We have that writer's two classics: *The Cloud of Unknowing* and *The Book of Privy Counseling*.[3]

Although he was a sophisticated theologian, well acquainted with such great thinkers as Augustine, Gregory, Bernard and Aquinas, this "Anonymous" did not approve of thinking while praying. He was not being anti-intellectual; **it was rather that thinking got in the way of contact with God. "Reject all thoughts."**[4] "God can be loved but he cannot be thought. He can be grasped by love but never by thought."[5] Anonymous was full of advice about what to do "if your mind begins to intellectualize."

Faith is "the substance of things hoped for." Hope is of the heart, or the gizzard, or as Jesus says it in the New Testament Greek, the *splagna*,[6] the guts. It has more to do with that scary ride in the wheelbarrow along the tightrope or that strut down Bourbon Street than it does with those whirling computers of the mind.

What changed Bill Wilson's life came not from his brain!

When intellectuals come into AA, a few of them parade their education to try to paper over their shame. Others get lost at first trying to figure it all out! Those who are lucky hear someone gently remark, "We've had a few folk around here who were too smart to make it. We haven't had anyone yet who was too dumb."

ENDNOTES

1. *Man Against Himself*, NY, 1938, pages 140-141. "Dr. Karl" was the virtual dean of American psychiatry during the decade and a half following World War II.

2. *Twelve Steps and Twelve Traditions*, Op cit, pages 29-30.

3.   William Johnston, editor, Image Books, Doubleday, NY, 1973.

4.   Ibid., page 9.

5.   Ibid., quoting Johnston, page 9.

6.   It has such a wet and messy sound to it when pronounced.

Chapter IX
Around the Bend

Fred has now been going to AA meetings for six months. He attended eighty-seven meetings in the first ninety days of his sobriety. Two of those other days his sponsor told him to take June to a movie. One night he stayed home in defiance and pouted, but he soon got over it, after talking with his sponsor.

Now he goes Monday nights, Wednesday and Friday at lunchtime, Saturday and Sunday nights. Monday and Saturday nights June goes with him. She goes to her Al-Anon meetings on Monday, just down the hall from his meeting, and Saturday nights they go together to an open AA meeting. On Tuesday nights June goes out alone to her home group of Al-Anon. They have to pay a lot of baby-sitter fees, but they believe it is worth it. As they see it, everyone in the family benefits.

Fred still attends his aftercare treatment group on Thursday night, but he and his sponsor, Ben, are trying to decide if he still needs aftercare. In some ways he has outgrown it. Not all of his aftercare peers are attending AA with the passion Fred is. It appears that some of them are not going to make it through the passageway safely. Ben points out how much Fred can "go to school" on their mistakes. Fred agrees to attend aftercare a while longer. He still fears breaking the contact with his treatment center.

At many AA meetings Fred hears the "Promises" read.[1]

> "...We are going to know a new freedom and a new happiness. We will not regret the past nor wish to shut the door on it. We will comprehend the word serenity and we will know peace....That feeling of uselessness and self pity will disappear. We will lose interest in selfish things and gain interest in our fellows. Self seeking will slip away. Our whole attitude and outlook upon life will change. Fear of people and of economic insecurity will leave us. We will intuitively know how to handle situations which used to baffle us. We will suddenly realize that God is doing for us what we could not do for ourselves.

He has already tasted some of "a new freedom and a new happiness" and he does not "regret the past" as before.

His invincible ignorance is vanishing. Still, there are parts of himself he can't yet accept. He still has some resentments and he has been advised these are very dangerous. He has heard over and over again how resentments got other members drunk. Charlie, a member of his AA group, talks about "throwing a drunk" at his boss. Fred still has resentments toward his own boss, who has an alcoholic wife and sometimes takes his feelings out on other alcoholics. Fred is also bitter toward the guy down the street he thinks poisoned their cat.

Fred has taken some consolation from the reading at the beginning of each meeting, which reminds him that "We are not saints."

Then he thinks of Bill the carpenter, who keeps saying, "I've got to keep green and growing. You either grow or go." Bill is younger than Fred, but he has been sober for over two years. Fred wonders if he is growing enough. He remembers something else they read at each meeting, that he must be "willing to go to any lengths" for his sobriety.

Fred and his sponsor, Ben, go to lunch to have a talk about Fred's growth. Ben wants to talk about his tomato plants. "You know I planted them and fertilized them. I staked them and watered them when it didn't rain. They grow real good now, fat and juicy."

Fred says, "Yeah, but how about...?"

"You're growing good, Fred. You've put on some weight and you stand up straight now. You're being watered and fertilized, but maybe it's time for some more step work."

"Whatcha have in mind?"

"Well, it's time you faced some of your character defects and the other imperfections we all have. There is a lot about yourself you'll just have to accept. Maybe you'll want to turn this over to your AA group and the God of your understanding. If you will further permit my gardening metaphor, it is time to trust the gardener. Now it's time to trust the program."

"Isn't there something else I should be doing?"

"Well, maybe there is. Why not read Chapters Six and Seven in your *Twelve and Twelve*. Then read them all over again. Okay?" (These steps concern first becoming willing and then asking God to remove our defects of character.)

As Fred read, the words at the bottom of page 63 jumped out at him. His "obsession to drink" has vanished. He has forgotten it, can't remember just when it went away. He has reason to be grateful to the God of his understanding. Although he has thanked Ben and other group members, it is only dimly coming into his awareness that God had something to do with it.

As he reads on he realizes he'll never be "white as snow"[2] and that his recovery from his defects of character will be a "lifetime job."[3] He will have to be "content with patient improvement."

Step Six. Were entirely ready to have God remove all these defects of character.
Step Seven. Humbly asked Him to remove our shortcomings.

Fred realizes finally that these steps are really about humility. As he turns shortcomings over to God for inspection and comment, especially his resentment toward his boss, he is both relieved and anxious: relieved to share the burden with God, anxious as to what he might hear in response. One guy in his group keeps advising others to pray for the very people toward whom they have a resentment! Fred thinks this is a bit spiritually arrogant, a little too condescending. Besides, he has a fantasy of his boss falling down the steps and breaking his neck. If he prayed for his boss he would have to give up that fantasy.

He realizes he must continue his conversations with his God, or meditations, as Ben calls them. Sometimes God will let Fred be. Other times he makes Fred wrestle. He reminds Fred that the way of blame is not the way of the spirit.

The time of Fred's brawling judgments has long since ended. There is new zest in his life.

* * *

AMENDS AND GENERAL LEE

Step Eight. Made a list of all persons we had harmed and became willing to make amends to them all.
Step Nine. Made direct amends to such people wherever possible, except when to do so would injure them or others.

As a part of his surrender General Lee had been willing to make amends: "The only dignified course is to take the consequences of my acts."

Although Robert Edward Lee owned no slaves and was opposed to slavery, he was deeply complicit in retaining the institution of slavery. He shared responsibility for the deaths of thousands of young men. Lee was on the wrong side of history. Part of that was the hand life had dealt him; the other part was that he had accepted that hand and played it.

Fred has been on the wrong side of history and part of that is the hand life has dealt him. He never sat down and decided, "I think I'll be an alcoholic, just for the fun of it. Just see how much trouble I can cause." Fred did not decide to have the Dopamine D2 receptor gene.[4] His DNA code helped decide that for him.

Yet Fred has played his own hand, his alcoholic hand. No one else played it. Someone has to take responsibility for his life. No one else can; he must do it.

The war is over. He can also see an end to the era of reconstruction. There are things Fred ought not to have done to others. There are things he ought to have done but never got round to doing.

Fred's Monday night meeting is called the Big Book Study Group. Members read a paragraph or two from the book, then comment on what they have read. Then others comment on the same passage. When it came Fred's time to read aloud he drew the following passage:[5]

> The alcoholic is like a tornado roaring his way through the lives of others. Hearts are broken. Sweet relationships are dead. Affections have been uprooted. Selfish and inconsiderate habits have kept the home in turmoil. We feel a man is unthinking when he says that sobriety is enough. He is like the farmer who came up out of his cyclone cellar to find his home ruined. To his wife he remarked, "Don't see anything the matter here, Ma. Ain't it grand the wind stopped blowin'?"
>
> Yes, there is a long period of reconstruction ahead. We must take the lead. A remorseful mumbling that we are sorry won't fill the bill at all. We ought to sit down with the family and frankly analyze the past as we now see it, being careful not to criticize them.

He stopped here, even though it was the middle of a paragraph. He thought a minute and then said, "Well, I am certainly the guy coming out of the cyclone cellar. It has taken me a while to realize how damned insensitive I have been."

He paused and wondered if he dare mention his feelings about disappointing his wife in their sex life. He decided not to, to talk about something else instead. He talked about being an absentee father to his children when he had been passed out so often. When awake he had often been depressed, humorless, irritable and wallowing in self-pity. How could he make amends for such things?

Later in the meeting another member spoke of his sexual failures as a husband, called it "brewer's droop" and said it was because alcohol is a sedative drug that over-relaxes the central nervous system. He added, "It just limbered me up everywhere, in places I didn't need to be limber!" Everyone had laughed at that. As Fred looked around the room he got the feeling the women thought it was really funny; the men seemed to laugh nervously.

He thought about talking to Ben about his sexual failures with June, but decided against it. These failures were not only during his drinking days; he was still having trouble since he sobered up. He remembered they told him in treatment this might happen for up to a year after recovery began. They said it was part of "post-acute withdrawal" from alcohol.

He asked his God about it as he was driving home from the meeting. He was not aware of hearing an "answer" to his prayer, but as he came home to June, he realized they must talk. After they got in bed, he brought it up.

Fortunately June had already talked with her sponsor about it, and understood it was very common among men in the first year of recovery. She had been told to be patient, that it was probably the body healing itself from the ravages of addiction.

As they talked, June listened to his anxiety and pain over his "failure" as a man and as a husband. She listened as he explained how he had a "disease" which affected his central nervous system. Just as she thought he might find relief here, he returned to his feelings of embarassment.

She did not know what to do and she prayed quietly but got no "answer." She just listened. Finally he was finished and she still did not know what to say, so she just said, "Hold me." He did.

The next night they talked some more. He was trying to work out his amends to her and the children about the impact of his prolonged drunkenness on all of them. Once he had slapped his son in the midst of an argument, but never Mary Beth. But he had often been irritable, impatient — especially when hung over — with all of them. He had too often wallowed in depression and self-pity. Worst — or hardest on them — had been when he was "out" for the rest of them, an absentee husband and father. He was not out of the house, rather passed out at home!

They held each other before they went to sleep. June told him there was little he could do but remain a sober father for his children. He told her that was exactly what Ben had said. They cuddled closer and went to sleep.

Three nights later they made love, not as successfully as they had hoped, but they were both sure it had been worth the try. A week later they tried again. Things were improving.

* * *

At their Saturday night open AA meeting Fred and June listened as the Promises were read. They came to the words: "We will intuitively know how to handle situations which used to baffle us. We will suddenly realize that God is doing for us what we could not do for ourselves." Fred turned and looked at June and she returned his gaze. Just barely preceptibly, so that only he could tell it, she nodded "Yes." His eyes half-blinked back to her that he read her message and very much approved of what she thought and how she felt.

They were well on their road to recovery. They had made it through the Donner Pass. Clear skies lay ahead.

* * *

All recovery boils down to three tasks. These tasks are very simple, but very difficult. Anyone who is willing to do them can recover.

1. *Accept the invincible ignorance.* Resolve to take it seriously. This means you have to become willing to stop trying all your old solutions, which haven't been working anyway.

2. *Get a Big Friend.* Find someone (or someones) big enough and strong enough to stay clean and sober themselves. They must also be friendly enough and willing enough to help you. A counselor may do for a start, but finally — because the relationship is professional — it must come to an end. Preachers and doctors may help some. They may be friendly enough, but are they big enough? What can they say to Leroy when he wants to get high on cocaine? Most haven't been there. The combination of the AA/NA group (especially the "winners"[6]), the sponsor and the God of your understanding are the best Big Friend.

3. *Do it!* Do what? Put the hammer down! All the way. Go where the winners are and do what they do.

It is the same whether you want to learn how to play baseball, master the violin or speak French. The people in France understand

French better than your high school French teacher, so go to France to learn French. The people at Julliard know — or know who knows — best how to play that fiddle. So go there. If you really want to play big league baseball, go watch the winners. Do what they do. Eat it, read it, study it, sleep it, think it, play it and work at it until you drop. And, obviously, if you want to get permanently sober, go where the winners are and do what they do. Read it, think it, seek companions who do it, go to meetings until someone suggests you've gotten down-right fanatic about it.

* * *

Months later Fred received something in the mail from a friend which came just when he needed it, and summarized everything for him. It also strengthened his resolve to keep on keeping on.

The Wicket Gate

Suddenly out of the mist, one sees a gate, sharply illu-mined by a light, that until this moment has been dim and hazy. As Bunyan said, over the gate is written, "Knock and it shall be opened to you;" Knock, however, only if you want the gate to be opened to you; the other side of the gate is called LIFE, and once you have undertaken the journey on that side, you have no choice but to live, and that is a costly process, a painful pro-cess, a process with the outcome unknown. On this side of the gate are all the safe easy outs, the painkillers — sloth, aimlessness, meaninglessness, irresponsibility — ugly words, perhaps, but such secure niches in which to curl up in a costless, embryonic sleep. Once you go through that gate, you have passed the point of no return. Though the journey ahead is a long one, you cannot turn back. One cannot return to not knowing when one has known; to not understanding when one has understood, to insensitivity when one has sensed. And as you walk through the Wicket Gate, you leave behind the possibility of ever finding surcease from the responsibility of your own sure inner knowledge — you are accountable for all you know and all you understand and all you are.[7]

Yes, Fred understood that he could — and might — drink again. This quotation provided no absolute immunity. He had seen others who had gone out and drunk again, and he had seen how difficult it was for them to return to AA.

Until this minute he thought he had never fully realized how profound was that little statement he kept hearing and repeating over and over again, "Just one day at a time." He was where he was supposed to be, in a meeting, and he was sober today.

ENDNOTES

1. Big Book, pp 83-84.
2. Ibid., page 65.
3. Ibid.
4. I use this Dopamine D2 receptor gene more metaphorically than scientifically. It may or may not be one of the "causes" of alcoholism. The point is Fred obviously inherited something over which he had no control.
5. Big Book, begins bottom paragraph page 82.
6. The term "winners" refers to those of long-term, quality sobriety who are widely respected in the AA and NA communities.
7. Quotation used by permission of the Educational Center, 6357 Clayton Road, St. Louis, MO 63117. It is an elaboration upon and paraphrase of a quotation from John Bunyan and the centerpiece from a course of the same name.

Chapter X
Passageway Companions

Based on my experience as a marriage counselor over the past twenty-five years, I am convinced that somewhere between the end of the second and the fifth year of marriage a major readjustment occurs. The romantic illusions the bride and groom had about each other give way to reality. Although this is depressing to both, it is healthy and necessary. When we first "fall" in love we see what we want to see in each other. After we have been married several years we have seen much in each other that disappoints or possibly even shocks us.

Some focus then only upon the negative and are ready to quit the marriage. Others are able to perceive both positive and negative attributes and begin to accept their partners as they are. When couples accept responsibility for this reality they are free to move into a whole new phase of their continuing adventure with one another.

Too many spouses try to avoid this adjustment, saying in effect, "This marriage isn't so good anymore, I think I'll have an affair." The affair can be with a lover, or a profession, or a hobby. It can also be with Ethyl, Mary Jane or Coke.

Some people go through a series of marriages and never come to grips with any marriage. A rich, permanent marriage takes time.

Fred and June have been marriage companions for sixteen years. For ten of those years Fred drank heavily. For almost two years now Fred has been in recovery. June is trying to follow him along the passageway, but she gets confused. Back when Fred got drunk every night, at least she knew what to expect. Fred has changed so, especially in the last year and a half.

As his companion, she is literally the one who breaks bread with Fred. After more than a decade of "Please pass the butter," "Did George tell you how he did on his exam?" and "Oops, I spilled the cream," their lives are understandably quite intertwined.

They intensify their dance as they join between the sheets together, then part during the day. Their dance has had its conflicts, but when they were skillful and sensitive enough they resolved them.

But when Fred placed another relationship between them, the marriage became a disaster. When Fred and June got in bed together, June could smell Ethyl on his breath.

CO-DEPENDENT OR CO-ADDICT?

I resist the word "co-dependent." It has become so trendy that I am never sure what people mean when they use it. I certainly wish to keep the "co-" part because of the companionship dimension, so for the time being I'll use the word "co-addict." If nothing else it escapes the stale, plastic-wrapped flavor of "co-dependent."

By "co-addict" I mean a companion of an addict who is obsessed with that addict's drug or alcohol abuse. June blamed herself at first, then tried to cure Fred and, failing that, tried to control his alcohol abuse. Al-Anon calls this insanity.

Alcoholics believe if they can keep enough liquor on hand they can be happy. Co-addicts believe that keeping liquor out of their lives can make them happy. It is a toss-up which of the two is the crazier.

As Fred became more and more involved with Ethyl, needing time alone with Ethyl, it is understandable how June became obsessed with breaking them up. She searched out hidden bottles and emptied them. She pleaded with Fred. She threatened to leave him.

Once she took their son, George, to New Jersey to her parents' home for three weeks. Fred sobered up and came to get her. Her parents tried to talk her out of going home with him. June believed this time it would be different, so back with Fred she went. For two weeks Fred stayed sober and June met him every night at the door with a kiss.

Fred realized she was more interested in smelling his breath than the kiss. He finally got mad and "threw a drunk" at her.

THE ANIMALS

There are many ways family members learn to cope with alcoholism. June has tried them all. First she begged Fred to stop drinking so much. He promised to "cut back" but he didn't. Afterwards she felt like a little puppy begging for a biscuit. Next she tried being a turtle. She grew a shell and learned how to pull her head inside of it. From there she could see what was going on but felt protected. She kept hoping things would change for the better. They didn't. Besides, Fred didn't like living with a turtle. June would have to try something else.

She became the Little Red Hen, the one who understands if you want something done you had better do it yourself. She did get a lot of things done that wanted doing. She made arrangements to get the roof fixed and have the oil changed in both cars. She started carrying out the garbage and cutting the grass. She hoped Fred would appreciate her, but he was too involved with Ethyl to notice.

So she became a weasel, a manipulating wheeler-dealer who is always ready to bargain with you, sell you on a deal. June tried bargaining with Fred, in hopes he could keep his bargains to cut down on his drinking. He just wouldn't, as it seemed to her. Truth is, he couldn't.

So she tried being a lemming, that little animal who will panic if you're not careful. Lemmings run and jump in the sea and drown themselves. Then you'll be sorry, won't you? So, a couple of times June threatened suicide.

Well, Fred did feel bad, got all shook up, and he certainly felt guilty. But guilt could not stop Fred's drinking, nor could pity for June, nor shame.

So June gave up the lemming role and tried being a lion. She snarled and roared. She threatened to report him to all sorts of people, including his boss. She told him what a lousy drunken bastard he was. He agreed with her, then went out to a bar to meet Ethyl.

Ethyl sedated Fred, made him feel better; his guilt was relieved for a few hours. Then as the sedation wore off he felt depressed, then ashamed. He came home projecting these feelings back onto June. He criticized her "lousy" housekeeping, her spending habits, her appearance, her sexuality and the way he said she "smothered" their son, George.

After he led the intervention on Fred, Mr. Babcock, the substance abuse counselor at the treatment center, had insisted she read Vernon Johnson's *I'll Quit Tomorrow*.[1] She had. Some words at the end of one of the chapters haunted her. She couldn't quite remember them. Her sister, Elaine, suggested she go back and read them again. She did.[2]

> The only difference between the alcoholic and the spouse, in instances where the latter does not drink, is that one is physically affected by alcohol; otherwise both have all the other symptoms. The dry is as sick as the drunk, except the bodily damage is not there. With every drunk there is a sick dry who is almost a mirror image.

June thought a lot about this.

Many of her friends felt sorry for her and believed she was an innocent victim — Fred's loyal, long-suffering wife.

Mr. Babcock thought differently. He told her no one could stop her from being a victim but herself. He said, "Victims choose to be victims."[3] She did not think much of that!

The next day she felt ashamed of herself again, blaming herself for his drinking. It was so confusing! She had tried *so hard* to cure Fred's drinking.

One day, after Fred had been in recovery awhile, her sister, Elaine, asked her, "Tell me about the Al-Anon meetings. Do they help much?" June replied, "Well, I've meant to go back to them but to tell you the truth, I just haven't had time."

The other end of the telephone was silent. June knew when her sister went quiet like this she was trying to find a way to say something difficult. Finally the reply came.

"Well, I'll be glad to go with you, again." Fred's counselor had emphasized Al-Anon to her when Fred was in treatment, but, well, Fred hadn't said anything about it in months and months. She had just forgotten. The finger was pointing at her. Her sister suggested Monday night. June replied, "Oh, I guess, ah, you know I have that school committee on some Monday nights, but you know...." Her sister was silent again. June said, "Well, I suppose I could manage it...if...if you think it's best." She did.

June asked Fred what he thought and he answered "great." She had some notion Fred might feel she was disloyal in going, but he said he didn't; in fact he had been wishing for months she would return.

She and her sister went that Monday, and then again on Tuesday night, over the next three weeks. Then June was ready to go on her own.

Al-Anon kept surprising June. She learned about the three C's of Al-Anon. She had not *caused* Fred's alcoholism. She could not *control* it, nor could she *cure* it. But she could get crazy *trying* to control it. They advised her how silly it was to try to make a scapegoat of Fred, or anyone else for that matter. She kept listening to what was said. It was several weeks before she could accept that she was not the cause of Fred's drinking. She was relieved, but also just slightly insulted. She wasn't yet sure why.

A male member of Al-Anon — Dora's husband, actually — said one night, "I used to think I was the cause of her drinking. And she let me think that, saying, if it weren't for me she would not have to drink so much. Then one day it hit me, who do I think I am anyway? I don't have that kind of power."

Over the next months June learned a lot: how stupid it was to pour out the booze and how naive she had been to believe Fred's promises to quit. She had asked him to make promises he was incapable of keeping.

Most embarrassing was what she learned about her "enabling" behavior. As others talked about their enabling, she saw how tricky this was and how hard it was to stop doing it. They had thought themselves loyal and protective as they covered bad checks, bailed their husbands or wives or lovers out of jail and called the boss to explain he was sick. One lady said, "He was sick all right, not like I tried to explain, with a bad cold, but sick with alcoholism!"

June thought of the times she had ridden home from parties with Fred while he was driving drunk. Not only had she been complicit with him in risking their lives, but she had given him the impression there was nothing dangerous or abnormal about his behavior!

They had been invincibly ignorant, thinking they were making things better instead of worse. An older member explained, "I couldn't see it for the longest time. My enabling just postponed her inevitable day of reckoning. You see, it just supported her delusion that things weren't 'that bad' yet and kept her from suffering the consequences, and kept her sick."

June finally spoke up. "But, I mean...how...how do you...didn't you just make everything worse? I mean, if I had let that happen, why it would have all come out in the open and...I mean, how embarrassing can you get?" Another lady said, "Yeah, well, you know, what the hell? Yeah, I worried about that for the longest time. Then I realized, to hell with what the neighbors think. It's *my* life, not theirs, and besides, the neighbors will find out eventually anyway — if they don't already know!"

* * *

As time went by, June began to grow alongside of Fred. She began to sport a new piece of jewelry her sponsor gave her. It was a butterfly. She did not have to be a worm anymore. (The butterfly is an Al-Anon symbol.)

She learned she was not as innocent as she had thought. She would need to work the Twelve Steps herself. She too had delivered "brawling judgements." She was reminded at every meeting how powerless she was over *anyone's* alcoholism.

On Fred's third AA anniversary, someone gave them a book. It was a present for both of them: *Hope for the Flowers*.[4] It was about a couple of caterpillars, Stripe and Yellow, and their separate journeys from worm to butterfly. The next to the last page says "The End." The last page says, "or the beginning."

The marriage of Fred and June had a brand new beginning.

*   *   *

Although her surrender was not as dramatic as General Lee's or Betty Ford's or even Fred's, June nonetheless surrendered. Her growth began in surrender.

Too many bitter widows of alcoholics long dead still cling to their ancient resentments. Parents of potheads threaten, reward, punish, bargain and then rescue their wayward offspring, hoping against hope for a change that never comes. They are too proud or too stubborn or too afraid to attend Al-Anon or Nar-Anon.[5]

ENDNOTES

1.   Op. cit.

2.   Ibid., page 30.

3.   Judith M. Knowlton, experienced substance abuse therapist and author, says "There are no victims, only volunteers."

4.   By Trina Paulus, NY, Paulist Press, 1972.

5.   Nar-Anon is to Narcotics Anonymous as Al-Anon is to Alcoholics Anonymous.

Chapter XI
Intervention

Gradually over months, then years, it became apparent how deeply addiction had ravaged Fred and June's whole family. It was not just Fred's alcoholism, but the addictions and co-addictions of other family members. Here is a diagram of the cast of characters in this drama of Fred and June Abernathy.

THE ABERNATHY FAMILY

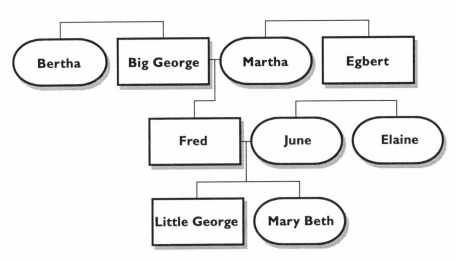

Little George is Fred and June's firstborn, named after his paternal grandfather.

His grandfather, Big George, is a retired executive with plenty of income who drinks a quart of Scotch whisky a day. His doctor tells him it is ruining his liver but Big George still plays golf at the club most every day, then stays late to drink whisky and play cards with the boys.

Big George and Martha have separate bedrooms. The old man doesn't play around with women anymore, but the damage has been done. The whole family understands the two go their separate ways, a virtual divorce within the big house on the hill. They all know you don't talk about any of this.

Martha plays the role of Lady of the Manor well, but she is intimidated by her husband. She is afraid he will disinherit her. He wouldn't do that to her, but he keeps her worried. He wants it that way.

Their minister has been advising Martha for years to try Al-Anon, but she is afraid. June invited her to go but she offered a flimsy excuse about not wanting to go out at night, at her age, "what with all this carjacking and so on these days, why George wouldn't want anything to happen to me."

Big George is very proud of his grandson. He has established a trust fund for "the lad's college."

Young George is fourteen and very bright. He shows leadership ability in his prep school, but is also a bit of a rebel. In fact his mother cannot remember a time when he was not rebelling. It is as if he were born that way. She remembers how hard it was to potty train him. The harder she tried, the more determined he seemed to leave those little deposits behind in his diapers for her to clean up. His grandfather always thought this was funny, showed "individuality." Big George always takes Little George's side.

Young George almost became a champion wrestler, but he lost in the finals. His grades went down from A's to C's. Then he got kicked out of prep school. Recently everyone read in the newspaper about his being busted for pot possession and a breaking and entering charge.

Martha wrung her hands. Big George called his son Fred up and let him have it. "Whatcha all been teaching that boy? Not that AA stuff, I hope!"

Fred and June's reaction surprised everyone, including themselves. They were initially as invincibly ignorant about their son's problems as they once had been about their own. They sent the lad to a psychotherapist who saw the boy's substance abuse as "adolescent acting out." For a while they told themselves "boys will be boys." June was talking with her sponsor about her son, saying, "Well, he's not that bad yet." Her sponsor replied, "He's not *what* bad yet?"

Young George drinks a lot of wine when he smokes his pot. Besides the fact that he may carry the same receptor gene as his father and grandfather, there are other problems that go with being the child of an alcoholic.

Young George judges himself severely. Because his childhood home was so alcoholically crazy, he has little understanding of what normal is. He is intensely loyal to his family — overly so, as are most children of alcoholics, accustomed to protecting family secrets. There were also times when he was taught his perceptions were faulty. He said "Dad is drunk" but his mother had corrected him. Dad was just "feeling out of sorts."

His dad was "no sort of common drunk." Then there were the times he'd taken on adult roles in their home years before he was ready. He tried to mediate the conflict between his parents, even though they did not seem to appreciate it.

Most confusing was the elephant family defense. It was as if a huge, brown, smelly elephant sat in their living room. You had to walk around it and pretend it wasn't there at all. When it broke wind you ignored it. Life at home was so much pretending.

Young George would go to his room and clamp the stereo headphones on and listen to his music. His parents deluded themselves, "I guess they all go through that." Their son devised ingenious ways to hide his pot and to vent the smoke so they could not detect it.

INTERVENTION

After two consultation sessions with Mr. Babcock about Little George, they decided it was time to act. Mr. Babcock would come to the house. He already knew young George from the family sessions for his father at the treatment center. June's sister Elaine would come too, but what about Big George, and Martha?

Martha begged off. Big George was another matter. He was so fond of his grandson and wanted the best for him. Yet, on the other hand, he might get so threatened about his own drinking they did not know what he would do.

Fred caught Big George off balance, on Saturday morning. He was in the family room talking with his mother when Big George came down for coffee.

Big George was not one for small talk, especially when hung over. He cut right to it. "OK, it's about Little George, isn't it?"

"Yes, dad, we want to get him into treatment and we want your help." Martha excused herself; she had some shopping to do.

"How can I help?"

"Well, Dad, you know how much he admires you and what you think; besides, he might try to use you as an escape route. He sees you as quite successful, a two-fisted drinker he greatly respects and admires."

"Yeah, well, damn! I...ah..I..ah...may have tossed back a few drinks, and a few too many sometimes, but I've never messed with that pot and whatever else these kids take these days. Besides — "

Fred interrupted him, "Look, Dad, we'll do most of the talking. You just be there. Just your presence alone will mean more than you realize."

"OK, but — "

"Just listen and go with the flow. I think you'll know what to do. Look, it's like closing a big sale and you certainly understand what that's about. We'll do the sales pitch with the counselor's help, but when it's time to close the sale you come in. If we can prevent him from wriggling out of it..."

"Yeah, OK, I gotcha."

Then there was the question of Mary Beth, his little sister. She was only nine. They were going to leave her out of it but the counselor said no. It turned out Mary Beth was more worried about her brother than they realized. She had found his bong[1] in the bathroom once and he had really blasted her. That wasn't like him. She was scared.

They chose another Saturday morning, a time when young George would likely be a bit depressed and vulnerable after the night before. His grandfather understood. They were all assembled, but the patient had not yet come downstairs. Mary Beth was watching the Saturday morning TV. The counselor reminded them of two characteristics that children of alcoholics usually possess: intense family loyalty and an overdeveloped sense of responsibility. This morning, that might work in their favor.

He came in, rubbing his eyes. He saw Mr. Babcock, but ignored him. "Hi, Gramps, whatcha doin' here this morning?"

"Well, uh, I — "

Fred said, "Son, we want to talk to you."

Young George looked at them, then sat on the ottoman by the empty chair. He stared into the warm fire in the hearth. The silence was uncomfortable for all of them; finally Fred broke it.

"We just want to ask you to listen to us, hear us out. Then when we finish, we'll give you plenty of chance to reply. OK?"

"Yeah, OK, what about?"

June broke in, her voice cracking as she tried to get started. "We're really worried about you. Things don't seem to be getting any better with you. You are depressed, withdrawn...and, well, uh, we've really gotten worried."

Grandpa just sat in the rocking chair and rocked, looking pensively into the fire. Fred broke in, "We do feel so cut off from you. You stay in your room most of the time you're home. You're in trouble with the law — because of that stuff you smoke — we've got you the very best defense lawyer, but still...look, Son, if you'll agree to go into treatment — like your dad did — things can go easier in his defense of you...besides...I really believe you need it."

June said, "That pot has changed you in so many ways, more than you even know, and that wine you're drinking — "

"Mom!"

Fred said, "You promised to hear us out."

"But I'm not an alcoholic!"

"Just hear us until we're finished, OK?"

"Yeah, OK, dad."

Mr. Babcock explained about what he called the amotivational syndrome that afflicts pot smokers, how they just feel blah all the time and don't have energy to do things they once cared about doing.

His mother continued, "We think you've lost control, just like dad did. You think you can stop, at least you tell us you can, but we don't think you can. We want to get you some help. Your sister is worried too. We all are. Mary Beth says she found your bong in the bathroom and really got grossed out." She turned and looked at her daughter. "You're worried about your brother, aren't you, darling?"

Mary Beth looked at the floor, then into the fire, then at her brother. A long silence followed, the she just said, "Please listen to them."

Fred picked it up. "I think the thing that bothers you most was when you lost that wrestling match. You know, and so do we, you're the best, the *very* best! We both know why you lost. You weren't in shape and your opponent was. A wrestler with inferior skill pinned you. You got pinned for the first time ever in a match. You cannot drink booze and smoke pot and train simultaneously. You know that and so do I. Pot and wine have snafued your wrestling, your grades, and we suspect they're even interfered with you and Emily Smith. You're not seeing her much now."

No one said anything for a few seconds. Little George started to, but Dad shook his head meaning no, then looked over at Big George. More silence, then Big George cleared his throat, "Haraumph," and looked at his grandson. Little George looked back at him with great big eyes. Finally the old man spoke, "You know how I feel about you, boy. You and me, right?" He held up his big burly right hand with the fore and index fingers squeezed together. He shook them for emphasis as he kept them squeezed. The lump in his throat made it hard to say what he wanted to finish with. "Please, boy, please, for me, if for no one else, do it." The old man's eyes were red and filled with tears. For a few seconds it was as if there was no one else in that room, just the two of them.

They had all had their say. Now it was Little George's turn. He wanted to try it on his own. He would have to miss school to go into a treatment center, and that wouldn't be good the way his grades were.

Waiting to be sure he was finished, his dad looked at him and asked, "Do you want me to reply to that, or did you want to say more?" "No, you go ahead," he told his father.

"I know about that one. If I hadn't gotten into treatment I would have lost my job. If you don't get some help soon, you'll flunk completely out of school. And you're depressed, maybe even thinking of suicide. I was, I sure was. Tell me you haven't thought about it."

"Yeah, well, I guess I did once or twice." Then Little George voiced his other objections. "Look, Dad, you drank for years. I've just got started, and look at Gramps, why he still drinks." The old man had been waiting for this one.

"I wondered when you'd bring that one up, boy. You are right. I do drink too much, way too much, and I ought to have my ass kicked for it. But — and this is a big but — I've gotten away with it, and so did your dad, for a while. But, Little George, it's too much for you. It is. Please do as they ask."

Little George looked down at the floor and said, "And if don't go?"

"We mean business, son. We want this for you more than anything. We cannot make you go, or if we manage to make you go we cannot make you cooperate. All we can do is make life as unpleasant for you as possible, and not reinforce your addiction. We are powerless to make you recover, but we can refuse to enable you any longer."

"So?"

"So, we will send your lunch money direct to your teacher. She has agreed to manage it for you. Your mother will drive you to school, no money for bus fare or anything else. Your allowance stops immediately. You will not be allowed to go out with any of your friends without special permission from us. We lock your stereo in the attic along with all of your tapes and CD's. Next we will let you camp out in the cellar while we search, scour, repaint and redecorate your room to suit what we think it ought to have in it. If you cannot be responsible for your room, we will have to be. Responsibility is a big thing in this family, as you know."

"Dad, you wouldn't!"

"Oh, yes we would!"

He looked at his mom, then his dad, then Gramps, then that counselor man and finally his sister. They all looked back at him, right in the eyes. It was very clear to him. They meant it. He was scared. Later he would be very angry. Right now he was trying to get the best deal he could get. He looked again at Gramps, to see if he had an ally there. He didn't.

So he said, "And what if I run, just take off and run away?"

Dad replied, "We talked about that too, all of us, including Mary Beth and Mr. Babcock. First, we don't think you will, that you are more gutsy than that, but we know we are gambling because you just might. But we cannot let that intimidate us. Your life is too important to us. Mr. Babcock has helped us realize we're already losing you as it is. What we've tried is not working. We must try something radical, something different."

Little George looked around at them again. They meant it!

"Well," said Little George, "it will take me a couple of days to get my stuff sorted out, to get packed and so on."

"That won't be necessary" Mom said, "We packed for you while you were asleep last night. Your favorite jeans, jacket and shoes are all clean for you."

After some more silence, a silence which seemed as if it would never end, Mr. Babcock said, "George, if you don't mind, and if it's OK with your folks, I'd like to take a little walk with you outside, just you and me. OK?"

"I guess so."

* * *

Big George said goodbye to his grandson and walked out to the car. He just sat in the driver's seat and watched Babcock and his grandson walk down the hill together. As he drove off he thought to himself, "I sure am glad he's going to get help....I wonder what my drinking has had to do with it all; I certainly have set him a bad example." As he drove along further he wondered if maybe he ought to get help for himself. Then he answered himself, "No, not today anyway; I'll have to think about it." He went home and fixed himself a Bloody Mary, a stiff one.

ENDNOTES

1.   A marijuana smoking device, has a large barrel and cools smoke through a pocket of water.

Chapter XII
"Those Meetings"

Our culture, especially as it emerged from Scandanavia and English-speaking northern Europe,[1] has used beverage alcohol so long that we tend to overlook its dangers. Beverage alcohol is a powerful sedative drug, with many of the same properties as ether.[2] Our lack of caution reminds me of the man who raised snakes. He got so used to handling them and so fond of them he got careless. While his pet mother cobra was having difficulty giving birth he decided to help her. Her bite killed him.

Yet we are simultaneously anxious about beverage alcohol and have been since Beowoulf's time, when chieftains slew each other in drunkenness. "Mothers Against Drunk Drivers" keeps reminding us how drinking can make us kill each other.

We have coped with our anxiety about alcohol by laughing, but it is a nervous laughter. Our comedians understand. I was born near the end of Prohibition, three years before the founding of AA in 1935. I remember those early comedy acts: W.C. Fields, Phil Harris and Red Skelton. They were followed by Foster Brooks, Jackie Gleason and Dean Martin. They made us laugh and gained our sympathy with their buffoon drunkenness. They talked funny, stuttering, mispronouncing words. All these comedians paraded ridiculous exploits and basked in their inebriation. By Dean Martin's time, Alcoholics Anonymous had come of age and was a force with which to reckon. When asked if he was an alcoholic, Dean would say, "Nope (followed by a hiccup)...nope, alcoholics are the ones who have to go to those meetings." It was still politically correct to laugh at drunkenness on display.

What about the people who attend "those meetings," and what goes on behind those closed doors? What is it about those who used to drink and drug and don't any more? It can all seem quite mysterious and some of the curious and skeptical have been known to pass on rumors, "I know they *must* drink, sometimes, somewhere." And then, of course, someone always knows someone who went to AA meetings and then went out and drank again.

* * *

Bertha was visiting her brother, Big George, and she and June had gone shopping together. June had been waiting for the question that came next. "And does Fred still have to attend all those meetings?" Bertha asked.

"You know," answered June, "Fred goes because he likes to go. At first I was a bit jealous, because he's so involved in it. I mean, you know, some husbands watch pro football and drink beer, but my Fred, he does a lot of AA service work; service work is their term for helping others."

"So, Fred is still out at night then?"

"Yes, but now that I'm involved in Al-Anon I go to my own meetings, and we go to some open AA meetings together."

"Well," Bertha replied, "Al-Anon is sort of the ladies' auxiliary of AA, isn't it?"

"No, Bertha, it's not. Actually Al-Anon is the real thing, every bit as much the real thing as AA and very important in my life!"

Aunt Bertha, not knowing quite what to say, stuttered, "Oh, I — ah, I see," which meant she did not see at all. June changed the subject.

* * *

Step Ten
Continued to take personal inventory and when we were wrong promptly admitted it.

* * *

Both Fred and June now understand how important it is to stop scapegoating — that the convenient habit of blaming others is dangerous spiritual business. Fred has heard over and over that resentment gets more alcoholics drunk than anything else. June knows that resentment will cause her spiritual condition to deteriorate.

As they drive home together from their respective meetings of AA and Al-Anon they talk. For instance, they talk about Fred's boss (with the alcoholic wife) and then about the neighbor they suspect of killing their cat. They remind each other that no matter how wrong their neighbor or Fred's boss might be, their Tenth Step inventory is about themselves, not other people!

They know what the Twelve Steps advise, that they "let go and let God." Fred is finding it easier to let go of the cat resentment, but then he doesn't care much for cats anyway, and he still laughs at the fantasy of his boss falling down the cellar steps. June will hold on to the cat resentment a little longer. Their sponsors have explained that these things take time.

Fred shares his gratitude that his "brawling judgements" upon the family have ended and things will stay that way — as long as he keeps the "plug in the jug." June simply nods yes and avers her gratitude that their silent treatment of each other has ended. She can't decide quite whom to thank: AA, Al-Anon, God?

Fred had not been able to give up his silent treatment until about six months previously. He used to come home, speak only a superficial word to her, kiss her on the forehead and turn on the TV. That was when June was still taking the posture that she was innocent of everything about Fred's drinking, and Fred was still so full of shame, guilt and bitterness. They refer to that painful time as the time of "the blaming," when they thought blaming was a solution in life. It is not that they have been cured of blaming completely — they are not perfect — but blaming is no longer a way of life.

As they continue driving and talking Fred says, "You know, the Tenth Step is about surrender too, almost as much as the First Step is, just a different giving up, a giving up of resentment."

They drive on a while longer in silence. They can do that now, comfortably. It is not like it used to be, when they didn't talk because each was so afraid of saying the wrong thing, wondering what the other was thinking but not daring to ask.

June had previously shared with Fred how she had felt when she finally realized he could not stop drinking no matter how hard he tried; she was stunned and felt guilty. She had been blaming him for what he could not help but do, drink out of control. This was long after she had accepted intellectually that alcoholism was a disease. She agreed with Fred that the few inches from the top of the head to the gizzard was a long, long way.

For their marriage to continue to improve, she had to continue letting go of her resentments. Al-Anon had taught her how spiritually dangerous it was to harbor them. She had outgrown the need to appear before the world as an innocent victim!

* * *

Steps Ten, Eleven and Twelve are called the maintenance steps of the program. The first nine steps get you into recovery; the last three keep you there. An old-timer, when asked why she kept going to those meetings, said, "Well, I had a very hard time making up my mind to stop drinking and taking those tranquilizers, but AA taught me how to make up my mind. Now I go to *keep* my mind made up."

Step Eleven
Sought through prayer and meditation to improve our conscious contact with God as we understood Him, praying only for knowledge of His will for us and the power to carry that out.

* * *

Claire is an old-timer in Fred's home group.[3] Both Fred and June are fond of her. She says she is not religious, but she is spiritual. Her prayers are fecund, like her gardening. She talks to God the same way she talks to them, about the "shit" life has handed her that day.[4]

She claims there are days when her spirituality is tested, when a child dies or a woman suffers abuse. She is cynical about churches and no longer attends. She sends her "offerings" to charities.

She loves the Eleventh Step, its focus on the will of God for her. Asked if she ever thinks about drinking, she said, "Oh, yes, yes I do sometimes." She went on to describe how nice her old favorite, Scotch whisky, would taste, said she could still remember the smell of it. Then she added, "But, you see, I realize that if I drank I might miss something special God has planned for me, down the road a bit."

Claire taught Fred and June her Eleventh Step breathing exercise, one she had learned at a Twelve Step retreat. She asked them to pay attention to their breathing. "For heaven's sake," she said, "don't *do* anything about it! Just let it continue to happen, just as it was happening before you took notice. The breaths just come and go, some bigger than others. They are like ocean waves coming and going on a beach."

Claire says, "When you think about it, it's wondrous!"

Claire remembered the retreat master had told them, "God made us from the clay, then breathed His life into us." She also remembered that when we die the nurses sometimes write "expired" on our chart, from the same root word as spirit, spiritual and inspiration. "So then I realize, every once in a while," she continued, "that there I am, right down at Wal-Mart in the garden department, looking for a bargain, and there is old HP[5] just pumping away through my lungs, keeping old Claire going!"

* * *

Step Twelve:
Having had a spiritual awakening as a result of these steps, we tried to carry this message to alcoholics, and to practice these principles in all our affairs.

* * *

Fred has made it all the way through the "Donner Pass" of recovery now. He has had his spiritual awakening, although there was never a single dramatic moment like the one Bill Wilson experienced in Towns Hospital. As he sees it, it has happened "as a result of these steps."

He is especially glad June has made it through with him. Their life together is now a brand-new adventure. They have begun to help others find their way through the passageways.

Fred loves to quote the Big Book now: "When all else fails, work with another alcoholic." It takes him back, back to see ungrateful, lying, self-centered drunks and druggies, reeking of bourbon breath and invincible ignorance. More often than not the new guy never really gets sober, but Fred stays sober and finds gratitude once again for his own recovery.

Twelve Stepping is the opposite of selfishness and self-pity. Isolation is even further removed for Fred as he sees the disaster zone in which an active drunk lives. Fred is looking into a mirror of what his life would have become if he had kept on drinking.

His "attitude of gratitude" is almost automatic. It is a nice feeling to have.

Fred has begun to see himself as his Creator sees him; at least that's the way Fred tells it. Others in AA saw it first, especially his sponsor, Ben. They could see his commitment and watch his gradual progress. They were patient, kept encouraging him.

They could see his charm, intelligence and emerging motivation, his sensitivity and warmth. They had already borne his impatience and irritability, his arrogance and selfishness. He was "not a saint" but he was already becoming an inspiration to newer members.

It was their Saturday night open meeting, the one with the Al-Anon members present. Fred watched the lady who had come to her first meeting, shy, trying so hard to hide her shame. At the end of the meeting it was Fred's turn to award the colored poker chips, the group's way of acknowledging members' length of sobriety. (Newcomers are given a white chip.) He looked into the new woman's face, then at the chip before he gave it to her. The chip was so new and clean and white, almost pure! As he shook her hand, then awkwardly hugged her, he was suddenly struck with the magnitude of what he was doing. He realized how he was regarding her, with so much potential to grow and become everything God meant her to become. It was just the way other AA members had regarded him when he came into these rooms. They had seen his potential for love and goodness. They had seen his potential and treated him not just as any old drunk, but as what he is today. He had become what he had been considered to be, good, kind and very lovable.

He wanted to hug her again, but it just did not seem appropriate. He wanted to hug some of that hope of transformation into her.

But Fred knew he would have to stand aside and be patient. He must "let go and let God," just as others had done for him. He could "carry the message" now, but he could never "carry the alcoholic."

*   *   *

So how could June explain this to Aunt Bertha when she wanted to know if Fred still had to attend "those meetings"?

She couldn't, unless she could get her to go to some Al-Anon and open AA meetings with her. This did not seem an option for today.

It is up to Fred, June and their Big Friends now. It matters less and less what Aunt Bertha or anyone else thinks. They are not yet sure of Little George's recovery and they take that one day at a time.

Mr. and Mrs. Abernathy are free now. They used to think they were free, back when they were strait-jacketed, hiding from the world in their invincibly ignorant, invisible purgatory. Now they really *are* free.

*   *   *

As they drove home in the rain, June said, "I like that new woman. We had a chance to chat at the coffee urn."

"Yeah, I saw you; think she'll come back?"

"She seemed serious. Did you see her talking with Claire after the meeting?"

"Yes, I did."

As they pulled up to the house it was raining harder than ever, so they just sat until it slacked off before going inside. Fred said, "You know, it just takes *so* many meetings before the miracle happens, so many ODAT[6] days just to learn the language, then to begin to change a whole way of life."

"Yes, it does. Well, shall we make a dash for it?"

"Yeah, you and me, Babe - let's run for it."

ENDNOTES

1. Vaillant, *Natural History* etc., Op. cit., pp. 58-63, and *Natural History Revisited,* Op. cit., pp. 59-64.

2. Father Joseph Martin's classic film *Chalk Talk* offers a compelling illustration of this.

3. Everyone in AA needs a home group, where they are partly responsible for the group being self-supporting and share responsibility for everything from cleaning up after meetings to paying the rent on the room. AA tabulates its census from home group rolls.

4. Actually her spirituality is not far removed from Biblical language. When Abraham "knew" Sarah sexually the Hebrew word was *yo-deh-ah*, the same word used when he "knew" God. In Phillippians 3:8 Paul says that compared to Christ, everything else is *skubalon*. The King James Bible translates skubalon as dung. "Shit" would be a more honest and accurate translation of Paul's language-of-the-streets Greek, especially given his contextual emphasis here.

5. AA slang for Higher Power.

6. One Day At a Time.

Chapter XIII
The Vision

Our faith can accommodate us as we are or it can transform us. A lot depends upon the faith we choose: a faith of accommodation or one of transformation.

Recovery must include transformation. Because addiction is often lethal,[1] accommodation faith is hopeless, paltry and dangerous.

A faith of accommodation enables the addict or alcoholic to continue in the old way, vainly trusting the willpower of old. It is as crazy as the story of me with the car jack. With accommodation, caterpillars remain worms; they never endure the cocoon, nor know the joys of the butterflies. Accommodation can only offer old nostrums in new packages. Accommodation prizes comfort and fears change. It offers cheap, painless solutions. It is hopeless.

Those who have lost respect for Christianity perceive it as merely a faith of accommodation, issuing its obvious platitudes, rife with hypocrisy. Matthew 25:31ff. translated into accommodation faith becomes:[2]

> I was hungry
> and you formed a humanities club and
> discussed my hunger.
> I was imprisoned
> and you crept off quietly to your
> chapel and prayed for my release.
> I was naked
> and in your mind you debated the
> morality of my appearance.
> I was sick
> and you knelt and thanked God for
> your health.
> I was homeless
> and you preached to me of the spiritual
> shelter of the love of God.
> I was lonely
> and you left me alone to pray for me.

AA's founders were grateful to have found Christian church resources in the Reverend Sam Shoemaker, who shared a passion for transformation with them. AA's co-founder, Bill Wilson, said of Shoemaker, "It was from him that [we]...absorbed most of the principles that were afterward embodied in the Twelve Steps....he passed on the spiritual keys by which we were liberated."[3] Sam Shoemaker was a popular Episcopal clergyman active in the Oxford Group and a strong advocate of a practical faith that changed lives.

* * *

Enabling is always accommodation. "Drinkwatchers," an attempt at applying Weight Watchers principles to addiction, was accommodation. Its newest incarnation is Moderation Management, a group which advocates "controlled" drinking as a substitute for total abstinence. As George Vaillant said about it,[4] "Nobody in the trenches is impressed with controlled drinking. Every time someone makes a good case, just wait ten years and you'll see they're wrong."

Transformation faith believes worms can become butterflies. But it requires being grasped, shaken and changed in the passageways. It happened to Bill Wilson and Bob Smith.[5] It continues to happen for the "Friends of Bill".[6] It happened to Isaiah of Jerusalem in the Temple, to Saul of Tarsus on the way to Damsacus as he was transformed to Paul, to Augustine of Hippo in a villa in Milan, to Luther on his commode in the tower and to John Wesley up at Aldersgate. It happened to Fred and to his wife June.

* * *

Today's vast spiritual markets hawk everything from New Age crystals and Hindu idols to classical Christianity and doctrinaire fundamentalism. People are seeking and getting confused in the process. Charles Nuckols of Emory University said,[7] "People feel they want something they've lost, and they don't remember what it is they have lost. But it has left a gaping hole."

A question one might ask amidst these spiritual marketplaces is, "Does this offer transformation or mere accommodation?"[8] If it is a crystal talisman or glow-in-the-dark statue for the dashboard it's superstitious accommodation faith. It promises a false hope, false protection as we keep speeding on the way we are. It's a lie.

Transformation faith is about changed lives. People have always been impressed with changed lives. They always will be.

One spiritual group consistently generates transformed lives. This group of spiritual amateurs has over 2,000,000 members and hires no professionals: no physicians, psychiatrists, preachers, priests or bishops. They own no property and avoid publicity. Their unwritten creed is powerlessness before a Higher Power they passionately refuse to identify.

This group is Alcoholics Anonymous. To their number have been added Al-Anon, Narcotics Anonymous, Cocaine Anonymous and Nar-Anon. They meet in rented church basements, firehalls, hospital meeting rooms and prisons.

As Frederick Buechner described them:[9]

> They could hardly be a more ill-assorted lot. Some are educated, and some never finished grade school. Some are on welfare and some have hit the jackpot. Some are straight and some are gay. There are senior citizens and also some twenty-year-olds...they are strangers who know each other only by their first names and almost nothing else about each other. In another sense they are best friends who little by little come to know each other from the inside out instead of the other way round, which is the way we usually do it. They do not know each other's biographies, but they know something about each other's frailties, failures, fears. They know something too about each other's strengths, hopes, gladness and about where they found them....[they believe their lives are] God's business because they all have God whether they use the word God or not. Even your own life is not your business. It is also God's business. Leave it to God. It is an astonishing thought. It can become a life transforming thought.

While they eschew creeds and scrupulously refuse any name for God beyond HP, Higher Power or God-as-I-understand-Him/Her/It/Them/Us, as I have observed them over the years they hold some strong beliefs:

1. The Higher Power is not fragile, like fine but brittle china. HP is solid and rock-hard strong, neither easily offended nor Green-Tile-Bathroom jealous. He can take care of Himself. One can dance and play before Him, argue and wrestle with Him, love and make up, know Him intimately. And God can be silly and laugh with us, at Himself and at us. Abraham discovered this millennia ago when he named his son Isaac,

which means "son of laughter." Abraham and his wife, Sarah, had gotten downright hysterical laughing at God.

2. HP's hardness is kind, "kinder than the softness of men."[10] The Higher Power joins with His own in their suffering and is mysteriously afflicted with recovering alcoholics and addicts as they are afflicted. As Ted Loder put it,[11]

> " ..and if you whisper softly of His gentle ways I shall scream of hard bitter days...life batters. Death grieves. I bear scars, I weep. I have questions deeper than questions, higher than heaven, and I have come to believe, passionately, that the worst sin is superficiality....the hammers of hurt drive me deep, for though it is dark there, I am not alone in it. I...embrace the abyss, the enemy I...kiss....I would like Jacob, wrestle till I am blessed by my wrestling."

3. As any good shepherd knows his sheep, how they look at their worst, what they smell like and how they get lost, Higher Power knows us. He knows us *well*, has the lowdown on us all, sees us as we are, yet looks beyond to what He means us to become. He beckons us into intercourse with him until we are changed into what He created us to become. In this passionate embrace souls are shaken and changed, transformed.

4. Higher Power challenges our accommodationist ideal — that our happiness comes from getting what we want — then bewilders us into believing our happiness comes from being grateful for what we have and that our only serenity is in His will. Recovering addicts believe this because they have experienced getting what they thought they wanted: bourbon, beer, cheap wine, martinis, heroin, marijuana, tranquilizers, painkillers and cocaine. But the painkillers nearly killed them, and took away everything they loved.

Mind-altering drugs are not all they left behind. As their guide, the Big Book, told them, "We...could not manage our own lives...no human power could....God could and would if he were sought."[12] Slowly and with one another's help, those who keep attending "those meetings" leave other old possessions behind: shame, bitterness, resentment, guilt, selfishness, arrogance, and self-pity.

Most astonishing is what they have "come to believe" about God's will, that what God wills for them is better than what they want for themselves. God knows them better than they know themselves!

For a few this transition was dramatic, virtually mystical, as with AA's co-founder, Bill Wilson. For most the spiritual awakening is more mundane and plodding, one slow step after another.

William James was the psychological and spiritual great-grandfather of AA. Thirty-four years before AA's birth in 1935 he unknowingly described AA's spiritual awakenings of the future. They would be, he said:[13]

1. Ineffable. The awakening "defies expression...no adequate report of its contents can be given in words." I have heard hundreds of talks where the speaker tried to describe "what it was like, what happened and what it is like now." "What happened" is still elusive, ineffable. I can tell you what the "drunkalogue" was like and what the results were, but neither I nor those speakers has ever adequately put into words "what happened." I have seen heads nod in understanding, but as James said, "One must have musical ears to know the value of a symphony."

2. Noetic.[14] The addict simply *knows more*, although not in the sense of acquiring more information. AA speakers are reduced to repeating inadequate words forcefully. James said they would enjoy "illuminations, revelations, full of significance and importance, all inarticulate though they remain." Others in the room have had similar, yet different, experiences. The task of passing on the message to others is ever elusive.

3. Transient. The warm essence of the awakening soon fades away. James said, "At most an hour or two, seems to be the limit beyond which [the awakenings] fade into the light of common day." This is why it is most important to remain in community with others who have recently had or are about to have a similar experience. Even addicts with profoundly powerful awakenings lose them if they return to isolation. James encouraged "when they recur it is recognized; and from one recurrence to another it is susceptible of continuous development in what is felt as inner richness and importance." "Those meetings" keep the miracle fresh. The newcomer is constantly encouraged to "keep coming back" and "just bring the body and the mind will follow."

4. Passive. The addict's "own will" is held "in abeyance" as if the will "were grasped and held by a superior force." The newly recovering addict is seldom aware of the change as it is happening. It must be pointed out by others, more experienced, who view it from their own perspective. This is the act of being grasped, shaken and transformed.

Fred came to like his sobriety. Others suggested his spiritual awakening had begun. He was dubious. Only gradually could Fred begin to see. It was just incredible that anything so special could happen to a "sonofabitch like me."

* * *

Again the paradigm of William James as elaborated in Bill W.'s *Pass It On*[15] (with editorial additions by me) is:

1. A sense of utter defeat; all human resources have failed.

2. Defeat is admitted, accepted! In surrender all attempts to justify, explain or deny addiction evaporate.

3. Out of this helpless, hopeless depth the addict cries out for help. This may or may not be in religious terms. When the help arrives, he/she follows the directions that come with it.

4. A deep sense of cleansing and forgiveness from guilt and shame follows, radically different from being excused.

5. Awareness of a new "zest" issuing in "lyrical enchantment, earnestness or heroism." Alcoholics and addicts find their "pink cloud." In their enchantment they understand themselves almost completely in terms of being an alcoholic or addict, as if that were all there was to say about them. This phase will pass, but they are entitled to it for now. Father Joe Martin encourages them to "squeeze it."[16]

6. A preponderance of loving affection toward others. Resentments give way to compassion. Recovering people reach out toward others who still suffer. The defenses of comparison ("I'm not that bad") are replaced with a new identity, as in "There but for the grace of God go I."

* * *

It has been a long journey from invincible ignorance and brawling judgments to becoming a magnificent, free-flying, multicolored butterfly. Alcoholics and addicts in full recovery know who they are and who loves them.

* * *

Thirteenth-century scholastic theologians sometimes get a bad rap, as if all they talked about was how many angels could dance on the head of a pin. Thomas Aquinas and Duns Scotus[17] were such medieval scholastics. They had an interesting debate, about whether sinners are better off having sinned than if they had never sinned at all. Aquinas said redemption meant sinners were restored to their former state of innocence. No, said Scotus, sinners are more blessed by having sinned and having been redeemed than in never having sinned at all.

Karl Menninger is reported to have said something similar from a psychiatric perspective, that recovering alcoholics get "weller than well," meaning healthier than most of the rest of us. It is in this spirit that we can understand something alcoholics often say about themselves: "I'm glad I'm an alcoholic," or "I am a grateful recovering alcoholic." It does not mean they are glad they made their families suffer; it means they are glad of who they are and where they are in their lives now. The only way they know to have gotten through their Donner Pass is the way they came.

I believe if I could resurrect Dean John Donne from his 17th century grave at St. Paul's in London and transport him into a modern AA room to meet Fred, then ask him, "Is this what you mean by a 'man made fit for God in that affliction'?" he would gently nod yes.

* * *

Traced back to its etymological roots, psychotherapy literally means healing the soul. Psychotherapy must include transformation. To have transformation, one must ultimately plunge into serious spiritual exercises.

These must include first a glimpse, then a growing awareness of ourselves as our Creator sees us, as God as we understand Him sees us. This means coming to believe, slowly, patiently, day by day, that He who created us will not only restore us but take us beyond to the fullness He had in mind for us all along. But it will require more than vision; it will require our full cooperation.

ENDNOTES

1. For instance death by stroke, cancer, suicide and accidental gunshot, poisonings, wrist slashings, overdoses of medications, household accidents, automobile accidents and cirrhosis, to name a few.

2. From the *Mid-Atlantic Community Educator,* as reprinted from the *National Nutrition Review, A Lenten Meditation,* summer, 1968.

3. *AA Comes of Age,* NY, 1957, see picture plates between pages 114 and 115.

4. *Time* Magazine, July 10, 1995, page 50.

5.   AA's other co-founder. Dr. Bob's transformation was more of the educational variety, "...because they develop slowly over a period of time." Big Book, page 569, Appendix II, which continues, "Most of our experiences are what the psychologist William James calls the educational variety."

6.   The affectionate code word for members of AA, Al-Anon, NA, etc.

7.   *Newsweek.*

8.   Admittedly some kinds of transformation faith are dangerous, such as Jonestown and Waco, but AA transformation is never exploitive.

9.   *Telling Secrets*, San Francisco, 1991, pages 89-92.

10.   Op cit, C.S. Lewis.

11.   In a sermon at his Germantown, PA, Methodist church sometime in late sixties or early seventies.

12.   Big Book, page 60.

13.   Gifford Lectures at Edinburgh, 1901-1902, as published in *The Varieties of Religious Experience*, NY, 1917, pages 380-382.

14.   From the Greek *noetikos* meaning "intellectual" or "related to or based on the intellect," Webster, 1977.

15.   Author anonymous, *'Pass It On' The Story of Bill Wilson and How the A.A. Message Reached the World*, AA World Service, Inc., NY, 1984.

16.   In his film *Chalk Talk* available through Hazelden in Center City, MN.

17.   From whom we undeservedly get the nickname "dunce."

Appendix A
The Twelve Steps of Alcoholics Anonymous[1]

1. We admitted we were powerless over alcohol—that our lives had become unmanageable.
2. Came to believe that a Power greater than ourselves could restore us to sanity.
3. Made a decision to turn our will and our lives over to the care of God *as we understood Him.*
4. Made a searching and fearless inventory of ourselves.
5. Admitted to God, to ourselves, and to another human being the exact nature of our wrongs.
6. Were entirely ready to have God remove all these defects of character.
7. Humbly asked Him to remove our shortcomings.
8. Made a list of all persons we had harmed, and became willing to make amends to them all.
9. Made direct amends to such people wherever possible, except when to do so would injure them or others.
10. Continued to take personal inventory and when we were wrong promptly admitted it.
11. Sought through prayer and meditation to improve our conscious contact with God *as we understood Him*, praying only for knowledge of His will for us and the power to carry that out.
12. Having had a spiritual awakening as a result of these steps, we tried to carry this message to alcoholics, and to practice these principles in all our affairs.

ENDNOTES

1. Big Book, 3rd edition, page 59, also in most other AA publications.

Appendix B
The Twelve Traditions of Alcoholics Anonymous[1]

1. Our common welfare should come first; personal recovery depends upon A.A. unity.
2. For our group purpose there is but one ultimate authority — a loving God as He may express Himself in our group conscience. Our leaders are but trusted servants; they do not govern.
3. The only requirement for A.A. membership is a desire to stop drinking.
4. Each group should be autonomous except in matters affecting other groups or A.A. as a whole.
5. Each group has but one primary purpose—to carry its message to the alcoholic who still suffers.
6. An A.A. group ought never endorse, finance, or lend the A.A. name to any related facility or outside enterprise, lest problems of money, property, and prestige divert us from our primary purpose.
7. Every A.A. group ought to be fully self-supporting, declining outside contributions.
8. Alcoholics Anonymous should remain forever nonprofessional, but our service centers may employ special workers.
9. A.A., as such, ought never be organized; but we may create service boards or committees directly responsible to those they serve.
10. Alcoholics Anonymous has no opinion on outside issues; hence the A.A. name ought never be drawn into public controversy.
11. Our public relations policy is based on attraction rather than promotion; we need always maintain personal anonymity at the level of press, radio, and films.
12. Anonymity is the spiritual foundation of all our traditions, ever reminding us to place principles before personalities.

ENDNOTES

1. *The Twelve Steps and Twelve Traditons,* AA World Services, NY, 1952.

Appendix C
Choosing a Counselor

If you, or someone you care about, are beginning this journey of substance abuse recovery, you will need guides and maps — and a friend, a "big friend." You will need a counselor.

Who will it be? Your family physician? Your minister? A pastoral counselor?[1] A psychiatrist? A psychologist? A clinical social worker or another sort of counselor, such as a substance abuse counselor?

While the "chemistry" or rapport between patient and counselor is crucial, it is also important to know something about the training and credentialing of your counselor. While credentials do not guarantee competence, they do measure a certain minimum knowledge.

MEDICINE

In the required curricula of many medical schools there is little training in substance abuse treatment, even though alcoholism and addiction are major causes of death in America. Two groups, the North Carolina Governor's Institute on Alcohol and Substance Abuse and the University of Virginia Office of Medical Education, are attempting to rectify this. However, as they describe the problem:[2]

> Current medical education fails to teach appropriately and adequately the subject of substance abuse despite well-documented effects of substance abuse on a significant portion of the population.... Substance abuse training is not universally integrated into medical school curricula and is not an integral part of primary care medicine. Inappropriate, though persistent, negative attitudes toward substance abuse and abusers and a resistance to expanding education in this area are primary hurdles that need to be overcome if training is to be better integrated into our undergraduate curricula.

Some physicians have educated themselves about alcoholism and addiction; others know their limitations and make appropriate referrals. The great problem is *recognizing* addiction. In defense of the family physician, alcoholics, cocaine and heroin addicts, tranquilizer junkies, abusers of pain-killers and pot smokers often deceive their doctors, trying to mask their drug abuse. Furthermore, doctors often tell me that patients simply do not want to hear the bad news that they may be addicted. Doctors who press patients about their drug use know they may lose a patient. Abusers seeking prescribed drugs float from one doctor to another, then to emergency rooms, eluding and using the medical profession.

Physicians are coming to recognize "Addictionology" as the medical specialty of choice in substance abuse treatment. Addictionologists are licensed medical doctors in good standing who have had at least one year's experience in treating alcoholism and other drug dependencies, completed "50 hours of Category I Credit toward...diagnosis and treatment of persons with alcoholism and other drug dependencies" and passed a six-hour ASAM examination. ASAM is the American Society of Addiction Medicine.[3] As of 1994 it had certified "some 3200 physicians from virtually all medical subspecialities."[4]

Psychiatry

Psychiatric competence in substance abuse treatment cannot be assumed. Psychiatrist M. Scott Peck has explained:[5]

> When I was in psychiatry training, back some thirty years ago, psychiatrists already knew that Alcoholics Anonymous had a better track record than we psychiatrists had. But we dismissed it as nothing more than a substitute for the neighborhood bar. We believed that alcoholics had what we called "oral personality disorders," and that rather than opening their mouths to drink, they would get together at AA meetings and yap a lot and drink a lot of coffee and smoke a lot of cigarettes, and in that way they would satisfy their "oral" needs. That was the reason, we psychiatrists smugly said, that AA worked.
>
> I am ashamed to tell you that the majority of psychiatrists, including those who are training right now, continue to believe that the reason AA works is because it is a substitute addiction.

In 1991 the American Board of Psychiatry and Neurology[6] set new standards in psychiatry, establishing the Committee on Certification of Added Qualifications in Addiction Psychiatry "to provide a means of identifying the properly trained and experienced addiction psychiatrist." Such qualifications are established by completing a "one year fellowship in addiction psychiatry" (or "5 years...clinical practice...spending 25%...time with addiction psychiatry patients") and passing a "written, multiple choice examination administered for 1/2 a day" indicating their knowledge of "evaluation and consultation, laboratory assessment, pharmacotherapy, pharmacology of drugs, psychosocial treatment, and biologic and behavioral basis of practice."[7]

Nurses

Two groups certify nurses for substance abuse treatment: ANCB and NCCDN. The Addictions Nursing Certification Board (ANCB)[8] confers the "CARN" designation, "Certified Addictions Registered Nurse" to those who have successfully completed its examination. Prior to the examination, candidates must have had two years addictions nursing experience. The National Consortium of Chemical Dependency Nurses (NCCDN)[9] confers the designation of competence on both RN's and LPN's. NCCDN requires more experience in addictions nursing and 30 hours of chemical dependency classwork prior to sitting their examination.

PSYCHOLOGY

On November 22, 1995 the College of Professional Psychology of the American Psychological Association announced a new Certificate of Proficiency in the "Treatment of Alcohol and Other Psychoactive Substance Use Disorders" for psychologists.[10]

COUNSELORS

Apart from substance abuse counselors there are five major traditions in counseling, and each tradition has its own procedures for licensure and/or certification: Rehabilitation Counselors, Licensed Clinical Social Workers, Licensed Professional Counselors, Licensed Marriage and Family Counselors and Certified Pastoral Counselors. Those licensed or certified have convinced a board of their peers of their competence in mental health counseling in general, but not of special competence in substance abuse treatment. Some of them, however, are working in substance abuse treatment centers. It is well for you to know how long they have been there, how much continuing education in substance abuse they have had and how much clinical supervision of their substance abuse work they have undergone.

CLERGY

Most clergy, even those with a three-year post-graduate Master of Divinity degree, have no special competence in substance abuse. Two significant exceptions are those trained at the Rutgers Summer School on Alcoholism (or Addiction) and those with several advanced quarters of CPE (Clinical Pastoral Education) in a substance abuse treatment center. Both categories of clergy usually display such credentials on their consulting room walls.

SUBSTANCE ABUSE COUNSELORS

In Virginia, my state, which is certainly not atypical of the fifty states in general, we have two recognized bodies which certify competence for substance abuse counselors. (The Virginia General Assembly passed a bill in the Spring of 1996 to *license* substance abuse counselors, although Governor Allen has not signed it.)

The Commonwealth of Virginia Board of Professional and Marriage and Family Counselors awards the designation of Certified Substance Abuse Counselor (CSAC) to those who qualify to take and pass the examination given twice yearly in Richmond. This certification is considered entry level.

The Substance Abuse Certification Alliance of Virginia (SACAVA) awards a higher level of certification, Certified Addictions Counselor (CAC), to those who meet its standards which include additional classroom hours and a face to face oral examination of a sample of the candidate's casework.

Two national bodies certify substance abuse counselors: 1. The National Association of Alcohol and Drug Abuse Counselors (NAADAC)[11] certifying at levels I and II, 2. the International Certification Reciprocity Consortium of Alcohol and Other Drugs (ICRC/AODA)[12]. ICRC also certifies clinical supervisors (CCS) of substance abuse counselors.

* * *

While these initials are confusing, especially to one looking for competence in substance abuse in an emergency, they do indicate at least a minimum level of competence.

ALCOHOLICS AND ADDICTS
IN RECOVERY AS COUNSELORS

My bias is in favor of the counselor who is also in long term recovery (10 years or more) and who still attends AA or NA weekly, still has a sponsor and has done serious step work. However, two important caveats apply here:

Alcoholics recovering in AA sometimes hear, "Son, all you need to know about recovery is in that Big Book and in the Twelve and Twelve." This *is always* true of one's own recovery, but it does not make one competent to be a clinical counselor to others. Interpersonal and diagnostic skills, biochemistry, pharmacology, treatment planning, record keeping and case management are among the many "skills and knowledges" substance abuse counselors need. When we train recovering people to be substance abuse counselors, we must occasionally confront their presumption that they already know all they need to know.

What happens in an AA meeting and what happens in a counselor's office are sometimes similar, yet often very different. In AA it is always proper to share one's own experience to help others. AA members help one another by describing "what it used to be like, what happened and what it's like now." In short, AA members most often talk about themselves. This is most appropriate, the way it is supposed to be in A.A.

Counselors come from a different direction, however; they must first learn to listen to and understand their patient! They are not in the therapy room to talk about themselves. Only occasionally is it appropriate for them to do so. They must understand, diagnose and develop treatment for someone whose story is likely very different from their own.

It takes a lot of experience, training and personal recovery to integrate recovery and counseling, and to do both well.

I suspect recovering counselors *can* have an edge to the extent they accept their alcoholism at a very deep level. As a result of such acceptance they may be able to accept others with greater facility. They may become more easily empathic; they *may* become more capable of tough love and harder to con. Often they can win the respect of their patients more quickly.

A CRITERION

An old story about Ernest Hemingway seems appropriate here. Once he was asked what made a great writer. After a lot of hemming and hawing he finally said, "All you need is a built in, shockproof, shit detector. When you can tell the difference between what is real and what is shit, then write about what is real, you can be a great writer." It seems to me this is also a good criterion for choosing an effective counselor. Can he be loving yet tough, kind, but with a built-in shit detector? Alcoholics and addicts are con artists. One con can spot another con ten blocks away.

Most of the best substance abuse counselors I know are recovering people. Yet a few among the very best are non-recovering, and they are extremely competent and effective.

ENDNOTES

1. Because of the First Amendment separation of church and state, government agencies do not usually license or certify pastoral counselors. (New Hampshire is an exception.) A nationally recognized certifying body is the American Association of Pastoral Counselors, 9504A Lee highway, Fairfax, VA 22031-2303.

2. Fang, Wei Li; Durfee, Michæl F.; Applegate, Stephen N.; Sdao-Jarvie, Katherine, and Lohr, Jacob A. *Journal of the Association For Medical Education and Research in Substance Abuse*, Volume 15, No. 1, March 1994, "The North Carolina Substance Abuser Project," page 34.

3. 5225 Wisconsin Avenue, NW, Suite 409, Washington, DC 20015, 202/244-8948.

4. ASAM Booklet of Information, 1994.

5. *Further Along the Road Less Traveled* by M. Scott Peck, page 139.

6. Executive offices are 500 Lake Cook Road, Suite 335, Deerfield, Illinois 60015-5249, (708) 945-7900.

7. Information Booklet of The American Board of Psychiatry and Neurology, Inc. entitled *Information for Applicants for Added Qualifications*, pages 10-11, 1995.

8. 4101 Lake Boone Trail, Suite 201, Raleigh, NC 27607, (919) 783-5871. Sandra Tweed, chairperson in January 1995.

9. 1720 Willow Creek Circle # 519, Eugene, Oregon 97402, (800) 976-2236.

10. In a letter to this author dated November 22, 1995, Russ Newman, Ph.D., J.D., Executive Director for Professional Practice of the American Psychological Association, wrote that the APA College of Professional Psychology was now offering this new credential. They can be reached at 750 First Street NE, Washington, DC 20002-4242, (202) 336-6100.

11. 3717 Columbia Pike, Suite 300, Arlington, VA 22204-4254, (800) 548-0497.

12. P.O. Box 1268, Atkinson, NH 03811, (603) 898-1516.

Appendix D
Choosing a Treatment Center

In the past quarter century we have seen a lot of changes in the substance abuse treatment industry. In the early seventies it was hard to find treatment. By the early eighties we were in the golden age of the 28-day, inpatient, "Minnesota Model" of treatment. The early nineties saw the demise of this format as the health maintenance organizations and insurance companies stopped paying for inpatient treatment. Today inpatient substance abuse treatment is accessible for some of the indigent (at taxpayer expense) and for the wealthy who can pay the $20,000-plus out-of-pocket expenses.

Many people recovered in those golden years, but even more went through treatment as a way to get employers, courts, social service agencies and family off their backs. A lot of corporate hospitals made "big" money. As one of my counselor friends put it, "They have killed the goose that laid the golden egg."

One unfamiliar with the mysteries of Twelve Step groups and treatment centers needs some way to conceptualize and assess them. I offer a metaphor.

ELECTRIC TRAIN METAPHOR

When I was a youngster, one of my favorite toys was the electric train Santa Claus brought at Christmastime, then whisked away after New Year's Day, then brought back the next year. The train ran on three-rail tracks and I pieced them together in sections, each just less than a foot long.

The Left Outside Rail signifies the medical and psychotherapeutic aspects of substance abuse treatment. This includes the necessary medically supervised acute withdrawal phase when seizures, delerium tremens and other perils may occur. This rail also includes individual counseling, group and family counseling and psychotherapy, which continues all during treatment and well into aftercare. This process involves both thoughts and emotions. As Dr. C. G. Jung said[1] "Ideas, attitudes and emotions which were once the guiding forces of the lives of these men [sic]" must change. He called it a "radical rearrangement." This Left Outside Rail process begins to unravel problems with self, family, employer, customers, colleagues and friends.

The *Right Outside Rail* signifies the educational parts of substance abuse treatment. A whole lot of information needs to be learned in a very short time. It is different from schoolwork; it must function very soon at fingertip level. This information includes most of what is described in the first thirteen chapters of this book and much more. It begins with the first penetration of "invincible ignorance" and continues. It must never cease.

The *Middle Rail* carries the electric current that makes the train run. Without it nothing else works! This rail carries the power of the Twelve Step movements: Alcoholics Anonymous, Narcotics Anonymous, Cocaine Anonymous, Al-Anon and Nar-Anon. *This must begin the very first day of treatment!* It must happen outside the treatment center, the real thing, "down home" AA. Patients must experience for themselves that "down home" AA and NA are always a little less than perfect. Twelve Step programs are not perfect; they simply *work!*

During treatment the addict is usually most dependent on the treatment center itself. However, by the end of treatment, AA and/or NA must have become as important to the addict as the treatment center. Most failures in treatment occur when patients fall into the gap after leaving the treatment center. They are facing the real world all by themselves. Like the woman on the flying trapeze, they need to be able to grasp the AA trapeze as they let go of the treatment trapeze. We want patients in AA the first day they are home, preferably accompanied by a temporary sponsor. *Every day of procrastination increases the probability of crashing with no net below.*

The Countryside Through Which the Train Runs during treatment includes what the Medieval Church called *sanctuary*, what psychiatry originally meant by *asylum*. Protection! Patients need some temporary protection from a world they perceive as alien and hostile toward them.

Paradoxically, some treatment centers are also a bit like a military boot camp. Patients do menial chores, must work very hard and are sometimes humiliated into the early stages of humility. Patients need some excuse to gripe. It is part of the fabric of the *esprit de corps* of it all.

* * *

Continuing Care, sometimes called Aftercare, is the last phase — yet like commencement at college, it is also the beginning of the rest of your life. Most important to understand is that:

MORE IS BEGUN THAN COMPLETED

Use of terms such as "graduation" from treatment programs imply one has completed one's recovery. Nothing could be more deceptive. *More has been begun* in treatment — even for the most motivated of patients — *than has been completed!* For a successful outcome from treatment the following, begun in treatment, must continue vigorously!

1. Regular AA or NA attendance, five to seven meetings per week.

2. An aftercare group which is provided at no additional expense by most treatment centers. Standard is an hour and a half per week. This is in *addition* to AA. This is not only in the patient's best interest; it is also good for the treatment center. Those patients who use it are usually the success stories. The magnetism of these winners is the best advertisement the treatment center has.

3. Active sponsorship means daily contact with the sponsor. Some well-meaning folk ask someone to sponsor them, collect a name and telephone number and put it in their pocket only to forget it. These unfortunates are not going to telephone the sponsor before their first drink; they just think they are. Only those who are used to talking to their sponsor every day are likely to call at such a time.

4. Daily prayer and meditation and "an attitude of gratitude" as a way of life and a primary source of sobriety. This component is difficult for some outsiders to understand. That it is "spiritual, but not religious" seriously puzzles some. I don't blame them!

THE NAVY

I was fortunate to begin my substance abuse treatment experience as a part-time member of the staff of the U.S. Naval Alcohol & Drug Rehabilitation Service in Norfolk, Virginia, in early 1973. First we were housed at the Little Creek Amphibious Base, later moved to the main naval base. Chief of Naval Operations Admiral Elmo Zumwalt had seen to it that we had the best of everything treatment centers could wish. Commander Al Croft was our commanding officer.

With Navy doctors and other medical staff, psychiatrists, chaplains, counselors and clerical staff, over 95 per cent of that staff were in recovery themselves. One of my colleagues, who became a lifelong friend, was U.S. Marine Corps Gunnery Sergeant Jim Holes. A former DI, Jim was a very tough, yet very caring, counselor. He personified the best of that *esprit de corps* mentioned above.

Standard treatment was inpatient for eight weeks (extendable up to twelve weeks) after detoxification at Portsmouth Naval Hospital. *Every night* the Navy bus took patients out to AA meetings in Norfolk and Virginia Beach. Our sailors and marines left treatment with first-hand appreciation for local AA and carried this with them wherever they went throughout the fleet.

Wherever he was reassigned — world wide — each sailor was given a CODAC, a collateral duty alcoholism counselor, who joined that sailor at AA meetings several times a week. Then they met regularly for their weekly sessions. Guys used to say, "Your CODAC knows if you're going to drink before you do." In those days the Navy's standard operating procedure was to give patients one chance at relapse with one more chance at treatment. Two relapses normally meant a general (less than honorable) discharge.

It was the best program I have ever experienced — anywhere. Unfortunately, today's Navy program appears to have less steam in its boiler.

* * *

As she explains in her autobiography, in April 1978 former First Lady Betty Ford began her treatment at the U.S. Naval Alcohol and Drug Rehabilitation Service at Long Beach, California. She went in like a trooper, refusing the "presidential" suite of quarters, and choosing to live alongside female sailors and marines just like any other old drunk.

Obviously Mrs. Ford was greatly influenced by what she learned from the old classic naval program. Later she went on to help establish The Betty Ford Center. According to Linda Sunshine and John W. Wright,[2] the Betty Ford Center "is the most famous rehabilitation center for the treatment of drug and alcohol addiction in the country." As Lilly Tomlin said onstage in her smash Broadway hit, *The Search for Signs of Intelligent Life in the Universe*, "How will there ever be room for all of us at Betty Ford's"?

As Sunshine and Wright describe the Betty Ford Center's program it offers either very intensive long-term outpatient (up to one year) treatment or a variation of the old "28 days"[3] inpatient treatment. As Sunshine and Wright were quoted in *Forbes Magazine*[4] "The Betty Ford Center is trying to play down its reputation as a celebrity center." The Betty Ford Center's address is 39000 Bob Hope Drive, Rancho Mirage, California 92270, telephone 800/932-7540 (in CA) and 800/854-9211 (out of CA).

* * *

Today most people will have to settle for an IOP, or intensive outpatient program, a program with less sanctuary and less *esprit de corps*. However, I think patients and families need to know what the best treatment looks like so they can at least ask the right questions about an IOP. What are its strong points and what are its weaknesses? In my opinion the very best substance abuse treatment available today is the kind physicians and nurses choose for themselves.

TALBOTT MARSH

G. Douglas Talbott, M.D. and Judge Juanita Marsh founded the Talbott-Marsh Recovery Programs for physicians, nurses, other health professionals, pharmacists and attorneys on a 55-acre campus at 5448 Yorktowne Drive, Atlanta, Georgia 30349 (800/994-0185). TMRC has all of the essential components: detox, campus residence, campus treatment, the mirror image program[5], two family programs and aftercare.

The sources for my evaluation are the literature and video supplied by TMR Center plus interviews with two of their successful alumni. One was interviewed ten years post-treatment, the other seventeen months afterward.

One said, "It was the most terrible experience in my life, yet I am grateful I had the chance to do it. I wouldn't have survived without it." What Dr. Silkworth (virtually A.A.'s first consultant) described as "deflation in depth" in 1935 is still a fundament. The alumnus described: "They throw you into an apartment with sixteen other people for the first week and you can't go anywhere — not even leave the apartment — without another person being with you. They break up your isolation fast." A community group decides when you can get off the buddy system.

Founder Dr. Douglas Talbott believes that alcoholics and addicts have been so busy "unpeopling" their lives that they are now "just where the disease wants you, for here [in isolation] you can die."

Most often the new physician-patient believes upon arrival that there has been a mistake made in his/her case. Yet TMRC virtually has his license to practice medicine in the palm of its hand. New patients seldom realize how sick they are, not even the ones in wheelchairs!

The 96-hour assessment and detoxification begins at once; detoxification occurs next door at Anchor Hospital, 5454 Yorktowne Drive, Atlanta GA 30349.

The Residence Program: Patients live four to an apartment, 16 to a building, "a bachelor's life" with professional peers in "a modern residential community within walking distance of the...campus." It is here that Talbott says "90% of treatment happens." There is simultaneous peer support, guidance from "senior" peers, deflation in depth, high-impact education, self-awareness training, and an environment in which one is likely to surrender to treatment. The cost of the residence program is about $1000 a month and one stays in it "as long as one needs to," on average about four and a half months.

Every Thursday evening they have what some residents call the "romp and stomp," where patients are held accountable for their attitudes and behavior. When a new patient arrives his group simply wants to know his name, where he came from, what he *used to do* (as if he might not go back to it!), what his drug of choice is and which apartment he lives in today. In addition to "romp and stomp" there are two other apartment group meetings per week.

The Campus Phase of treatment begins "when you come out of detox," and "you are still stupefied." Patients are kept in this phase from six to eight weeks, until staff decides "if you are talking like a real person yet." This phase of treatment goes on five days a week, from 8:30 a.m. until 3:00 p.m. and includes counseling and psychotherapy individually and in groups, AA meetings, lectures, films, educational videos and study groups.

Cost for the Campus Phase is about $6000 depending on how long patients need it. Patients have compared it to a marine boot camp. It is the simple things that are the most difficult to learn, often *because* they are so obvious. Some examples are: how to live one day at a time, that the first drink is the one that gets you drunk, that you must surrender to win, and that "we" power, not willpower, is the way to recovery.

The Mirror Image Program is the second major phase of treatment where physician-patients work as "counselor-trainees" in another Atlanta area treatment center. This phase averages 18 to 20 weeks and costs about $90 per day. TMRC patients "see themselves, and become aware of the impact of their disease in all aspects of their lives. In this way, they 'mirror' off these patients." As one alumnus put it, we could "already begin to hear the difference between what's going on back at the residence and what [we were] hearing here."

Although patients are rarely aware of it at the time, they are now doing, in embryonic form, the substance of AA Twelfth Step work. Under very carefully monitored conditions they are already doing what the *Big Book* describes as "when all else fails, work with another alcoholic."

Later in the day they will "process" their experience of the day with a supervisor or senior resident back at the residence apartment. Stripped of virtually all medical authority, physicians can not only learn about their disease in depth, they can also learn some humility.

The Family Program begins with a monthly, four-day Family Workshop or the four-day Extended Family Workshop (a real "crash course") and each costs $750 including counseling, psychotherapy, drug testing and physical examination. The Family Program places strong emphasis on continuing Al-Anon participation.

Aftercare is where patients learn what to take back home and there is a *lot* to take home:

1. The telephone: "Regular calls every day of my working week to see whether I have to have a random urine screen for drugs and/or alcohol" as one alumnus said. Both former TMRC patients have sponsors with whom they speak regularly. One said "I haven't questioned these [aftercare standards], I've just done them."

2. Regular AA and NA attendance. Both alumni attend three or more AA meetings per week.

3. Weekly Caduceus Club meetings. Created originally in Georgia as a kind of state-wide aftercare for TMRC, Caduceus is spreading throughout the country and is a bridge to AA and NA for health care professionals. Both alumni friends of mine attend Caduceus on Monday nights.

4. Regular physical exercise.

5. Regular rest and leisure. It is important to experience play and to learn to look forward to fun which is not drug or alcohol associated.

6. Regular honest and open talk with family.

7. The daily prayer and meditation of Step Eleven.

8. The daily moral inventory of Step Ten.

I asked one of my friends, the most recent of the TMRC alumni, about the cost. He said it had cost him over $20,000, not to mention the time away from his medical practice. In reply to my question, "Was it worth it?" He replied, "Oh yes, TMRC is a bargain when you think about it." He went on to explain that since returning to his practice he is doing as well as the year before he left and working fewer hours to do it. He has ample time to do his AA and aftercare, have leisure with his family and practice medicine.

EXTRAPOLATIONS

I realize that possibly you cannot afford TMRC and you cannot find an affordable 28-day inpatient program (or one your insurance will cover). What can you do? You may have to settle for an Intensive Outpatient Program. You *can* ask some questions. Make the rounds; ask about several of them until you are better informed about your best options. You can begin by asking about the counselors on the staff in the light of the criteria in Appendix C. You will also kneed to know:

1. What is the actual day-to-day relationship of the IOP to AA and NA? *Do not* settle for such as "Oh, we think AA is very important" or even "I'm an AA member myself." You will want to know what percentage of their patients are counted as "successful completions" but are not yet attending AA five to seven times per week in addition to the IOP! Patients in this category seriously undermine the credibility, reliability and validity of the IOP! You may hear a lot of excuses from either patients or staff. The road to continued relapse and drunkenness is paved with excuses.

2. How many patients have a sponsor, at least a temporary one, by the third week? Patients will complain they are rushed, and so they are, possibly. Yet the whole process has been unnaturally and unrealistically shortened by the HMO's and Third Party Management people. You've got to get the best program you can! Unfortunately, sometimes those at the HMO scarcely know what they are approving or declining. Are they merely graduate students or are they qualified as substance abuse counselors themselves?

3. Ask about the didactic component of the program. You are entitled to know which subjects are covered, for how many hours, by whom and with what experience. How much is covered by mere videotape lectures and how much with real, live lecturers who interact with patients?

4. What is the ratio of former patients attending Aftercare or Continuing Care? If this ratio is below 20%, or if you get an evasive answer, beware!

5. Take your shit detector along with you. Keep it turned on.

6. What about the family program? Is there one? What percentage of patients and families attend? Ask if you can go have a look for yourself.

Good luck. Private substance abuse treatment corporations are in business to make money. They must report to stockholders. They have an extensive network of marketing agents, sometimes more sales people than clinicians. You need to meet some of their clinicians!

ENDNOTES

1. Big Book, Ibid., page 27.
2. *The 100 Best Treatment Centers For Alcoholism and Drug Abuse,* Avon Books, NY, 1988, pages 73- 76.
3. Ibid., page 75.
4. Ibid., page 73.
5. see page 142.

Appendix E
Interventions and Coercions

I have made the point that we cannot make an alcoholic or drug addict do anything. However, *the right kind of pressure applied at the right time by the right people can sometimes raise the bottom* so that the denial system can begin to collapse. Sometimes we can help midwife a surrender. Sometimes the surrender process has already begun inside the addict, although we may not know it. Afraid of yet another failure, he dared not tell anyone what he was thinking!

The conventional wisdom is that we must wait until alcoholics "hit bottom" before we can help. However, recent research indicates that we should re-examine this assumption. The Group for the Advancement of Psychiatry Report No. 137 says[1] that based upon studies done by Beaumont and Alsop,[2] "*Self-referral (is) associated with poor outcome.*" This is explained by the Committee on Government Policy. They say[3] that alcoholics and addicts "deny, connive, manipulate, deceive themselves and others and behave in the service of their addiction" in ways "generally unappreciated by clinicians and employee supervisors." They "escape a potential problem" by appearing more cooperative than they truly are. Alcoholics are not stupid. They have heard, just as most everyone else has, that "admitting you have a problem is half the problem." Their unspoken message is clear in self-referral, "My, aren't I good? I've already done *half of my recovery*. Surely you would not begrudge my having a few drinks here at halftime, would you?"

INTERVENTION

Intervention is a process invented by Vernon Johnson[4] and subsequently promoted by the Johnson Institute. It is utilized by most treatment centers. Johnson's genius was manifest in his realization that: 1) Intervention in a less formal style was already occurring in most cases of successful recovery. 2) "Even at his sickest, [the alcoholic] is capable of accepting some useful portion of reality, *if that reality is presented to him in forms he can receive*." 3) If we breach the line of the alcoholic's defenses we must not back off, but go relentlessly on, deeper into the defenses until "I'm not hurting anyone but myself" becomes something like, "Help me; I had no idea I had hurt so many people so much."

The standards for an intervention as developed by Johnson are:[5]

1. "Meaningful persons, persons who exert real influence upon the sick person, must present the facts." Talbot and Gallegos[6] add that this includes "family, employer/employees, friends, church, legal and financial advisors." Probably most crucial for physicians are representatives from the State Medical Society's Impaired Physicians Program.[7]

2. "The data presented should be specific and descriptive of events which have happened or conditions which exist. 'I was there when you insulted our client at lunch, and it was obvious to both the client and to me that you'd had too many,' or 'The word around the office is not to send you clients after lunch.'"

    Such specific events are harder for the alcoholic to counterattack than broad value judgements such as "You drink too much." Even "I am worried about your drinking" has more clout than that. After being counterattacked for saying "I'm worried about your drinking," I can still respond, "Well, OK, but in spite of what you say I am still worried." The alcoholic *still* has to cope with my worry. Even though he may express contempt for me at the moment, I have probably gotten through to him.

3. "The tone of the confrontation should not be judgmental." The data should show empathy, care and concern. However, despite how careful the intervention team is, they will probably be *accused* of being judgmental.

4. "The chief evidence should be tied to drinking wherever possible." If you remind an alcoholic that he has been depressed a lot lately, he may tell you, "Of course, that's why I'm drinking so much. I need to get to the bottom of my depression so that I can stop drinking." More directly tied to drinking is a statement like, "After that, you turned up that vodka bottle and drained it. Then you got behind the wheel and roared off, leaving gravel flying everywhere. Julia says you were driving over 100 miles an hour in spite of her pleas to stop."

5. "The evidence of behavior should be presented in some detail, to give the sick person a panoramic view of himself ....Sound movies or tapes of some of his drinking episodes will do it best." More likely you will have to construct a panoramic word picture. If he cannot get the big picture as you all see it, the alcoholic will try to make it seem as if the events you describe are mere exceptions in his drinking life.

6. "The goal of the intervention, through the presentation of this material, is to have him *see and accept enough reality* so that, however grudgingly, he can accept in turn his need for help." Talbot and Gallegos add,[8] "The goals and objectives must be clearly defined by everyone in the intervention." For instance, interveners are not there to extract more promises to quit drinking but to get the potential patient into treatment. Nor is the intervention team there to punish, although some participants may come with mixed motives which are outside their awareness. Team members who are themselves "co-dependent" may be on a self-appointed crusade to punish alcoholics. Other co-dependents may still be enabling, willing to settle for promises to quit, still believing the drunk could do it, if he just would! As Talbot and Gallegos[9] put it, "It may be necessary for the leaders to eliminate some team members who cannot or will not be constructive."

7. Leave the alcoholic some dignity of choice. In my opinion this is the most neglected of the cardinal points made by Vernon Johnson in 1973. Although the bags are packed, the plane ticket purchased and reservations made at the treatment center, still there must be some way to allow him some dignity. This may involve a choice between treatment centers, or even the choice to "try it on my own" for three weeks under closely monitored conditions with mutually agreeable, measurable criteria for total abstinence. With vague criteria to measure success, the alcoholic will slip by you every time. In such an instance the patient agrees *in writing* to go into treatment immediately if he fails!

    Experience with intervention has accumulated over the past decade and a half. Talbot and Gallegos add two more points:

8. "Rehearsals on two or three occasions will be required to allow...members...to know their roles." Unfortunately some members *think* they know more than they do! Others understand the principles intellectually but are not yet capable of doing them!

9. "The process should not be hurried." It takes time.

Finally, *expect the unexpected*. Some of the most well-prepared interventions I have administered have failed to get the alcoholic into treatment; conversely, some of the most ill prepared have issued in a successful outcome. Like all else in this business, we need to know when to turn this over to the Higher Power.

JUDGES AND POLICE

What about those whose substance abuse results in their violation of our laws? Legally, we can do more than we are doing now. Barbara Walters said,[10] "Study after study shows treatment programs without jail time are no more effective than license suspension." It is easy to forget how acculturated judges are. They are influenced from infancy by the same jokes about drunks that the rest of us find amusing. Many of them drink socially themselves, can control it and do not understand why others cannot. A few of them are drinking alcoholics. We do not have anyone to make lawyers and judges out of but *people*, and *people* — all of them — are subject to distortions of perception concerning addiction.

Barbara Walters and Candy Lightner (founder of MADD, Mothers Against Drunk Drivers) discussed some of these legal issues on national TV. They spoke of Eugene Standerford, a vivid personification of the problem and an embarrassment to the legal system.

Standerford has had thirteen drunk driving arrests in Texas alone. He has had his driver's license suspended eight times. After 26 years of driving drunk he was still at it. "Judges are real lenient," said Candy Lightner in 1994. He killed Candy Lightner's daughter while he was driving drunk in 1980. Ms. Lightner is obviously very disillusioned. She said, "The man who killed my daughter can never own a gun. But he can still have a car and he can still get a driver's license." In Wisconsin after his seventh drunk driving arrest — with the death of the Lightner girl in his past — all he received as punishment was a mere $500 fine and a license suspension. "Some states wipe the record clean three years after the last conviction."[11]

Judges declare so much previous trial evidence "inadmissible," creating a fictitious history of the accused for presentation before the jury. "Juries in drunk driving cases tend to see a victimless crime." Richard Alpert, a prosecutor interviewed by *Turning Point*, said, "Like some drunken Energizer bunny he keeps going and going and going."

LEGAL COERCIONS WE COULD USE

1. Drunk drivers could be forced to face their disabled victims in a controlled, therapeutic interview. Once I was able to manage this in my practice. It was fifteen years ago and I see the offender several times a year. I am convinced he still abstains from alcohol completely.

2. Col. Warren Davies, a state police commander, was interviewed by Barbara Walters. He said, "We [can] have a trooper come and put the bar—the club—across your steering wheel for 30, 60, 90 days at the order of the judge. And then, after so many violations, then we [can] take the car."

3. Walters offered, "Judges can order an interlock device installed, a breathalizer that will not allow ingnition if the driver has been drinking." I believe this should be at the driver's expense—not the taxpayer's. If he cannot afford this device he can walk or ride the bus! He is *already* resourceful enough to get whiskey or cocaine if he wants it. Let him be as resourceful with his transportation!

4. Clifford Peacock, Ph.D., of the Alcohol Research Group at the University of Edinburgh, quotes[12] P. Davies and D. Walsh:[13] "Much that passes for health education concentrates on negating the values and images portrayed in alcohol advertising." We *could* abolish advertising for beverage alcohol. This would modify the mindset in many persons who believe beverage alcohol consumption is benign. We could — if we would — abolish this advertising, if we were "willing to go to any lengths."

5. Clifford Peacock says,[14] "Penalties...are most effective when they are certain and swift....[when they are not]...drinkers...become reinforced in the belief that they are able to elude detection."

* * *

As the Group for the Advancement of Psychiatry has indicated, most alcoholics and addicts are not going into serious treatment until they have to. This is not inconsistent with AA philosophy. Nearly every AA meeting in the United States opens with the words "If you want we have and are ready to go to any length to get it, then you are willing to follow certain steps."[15]

Our whole society, in fact, enables alcoholics with its permissiveness and constant bending over backwards to guarantee "rights" to drivers like Eugene Standerford. Meanwhile drunken drivers are killing us off one by one. Drunken drivers seriously threaten our "life, liberty and the pursuit of happiness."

ENDNOTES

1. *Forced Into Treatment,* American Psychiatric Press, Inc., Washington, DC, 1994, pages 15-17.

2. *British Journal of Addiction* 79:315-318, 1984, "An Industrial Alcohol Policy: the Characteristics of Worker Success".

3. Op. cit.

4. *I'll Quit Tomorrow,* Op. cit.

5. Ibid., pages 49-51.

6. *Addiction and Recovery* magazine, article by G. Douglas Talbot and Karl V. Gallegos, September 1990.

7. Ibid.

8. Ibid.

9. Ibid.

10. ABC News "Turning Point" Transcript # 141, Copyright 1994, *Journal Graphics,* 1535 Grant Street, Denver, CO 80203 (303) 831-6400, page 7.

11. Ibid, *Journal Graphics,* Walters speaking.

12. *International Journal of Addictions,* 27(2), 187-208, 1992, page 198.

13. *Alcohol Problems and Alcohol Control in Europe,* 1983, Croom Helm, London.

14. Op. cit., page 23.

15. Big Book, page 58.

Bibliography

Allison, C. Fitzsimmons, *Fear, Love and Worship*, Seabury Press, Greenwich, CT, 1962.

Allison, C. Fitzsimmons, *Guilt, Anger and God*, A Crossroad Book, NY, 1972.

Allison, C. Fitzsimmons, *The Rise of Moralism*, Seabury Press, NY, 1966.

Anonymous, *Alcoholics Anonymous*, AA World Services, Inc., NY, 3rd Edition, 1976.

Anonymous, *The Cloud of Unknowing*, edited by William Johnson, Image Books, NY, 1973.

Anonymous, *Narcotics Anonymous*, NA World Services, Inc., Van Nuys, CA, 1982.

Anonymous, *"Pass It On,"* AA World Services, Inc. NY, 1984.

Anonymous, *Twelve Steps and Twelve Traditions*, AA World Services, Inc., NY, Forty-fifth printing, 1991.

Anonymous, *Alcoholics Anonymous Comes of Age: A Brief History of A.A.*, AA World Services, Inc., NY, 1957.

Blum, Kenneth; Noble, Ernest P; Sheridan, Peter J; Montgomery, Anne; Ritchie, Terry; Jugadeeswaran, Pudur; Nogami, Harou; Briggs, Arthur and Cohn, Jay, *Journal of the American Medical Association*, Vol. 263. No. 15, pp. 2055-2060, April 18, 1990, "Allelic Association of Human Dopamine D2 Receptor Gene in Alcoholism."

Blum, Kenneth & Briggs, Arthur. *Biogenic Amines*, Vol. 5, No. 6, pp. 527-533, 1988, "Opiod Peptides and Genotypic Responses to Ethanol."

Bondi, Roberta, *Weavings*, Vol. IX, No. 5, Sept/Oct 1994, "The Green Tiled Bathroom," pp. 6-27, Upper Room, Nashville, 1994.

Bondi, Roberta, *Memories of God*, Abingdon Press, Nashville, 1995.

Buechner, Frederick, *Telling Secrets*, Harper San Francisco, 1991.

Cashaw, J.L; Geraghty, C.A; McLaughlin, B.R. and Davis, V.E. *Journal of Neuroscience Research* 18:497-503 (1987), "Effect of Acute Ethanol Administration on Brain Levels of Tetrahydropapaveroline in L-dopa-treated Rats."

Chappelle, Frederick; Durham, Thomas; Landerman, Donna; Powell, David J; Siembab, Lauren and Simonds, Nancy, *Counselor Development: A Training Manual for Drug and Alcohol Abuse Counselors*, ETP, Inc., Windsor, CT, 1994.

Collins, Michæl; Neny, Ung-Chhun; Cheng, Bhe; and Pronger, Debra, *Journal of Neurochemistry*, Vol. 55, No. 5, 1990, "Brain and Plasma Tetrahydroisoquinolines in Rats: Effects of Chronic Ethanol Intake and Diet."

Committee on Government Policy, *Forced Into Treatment: The Role of Coercion in Clinical Practice,* American Psychiatric Press, Washington, DC, 1994.

Fang, Wei; Durfee, Michæl F; Applegate, Stephen N; Sdao-Jarvie, Katherine and Lohr, Jacob A, *Journal of the Association For Medical Education and Research in Substance Abuse*, The North Carolina Substance Abuse Project. Vol. 15, No. 1, March 1994.

Foote, Shelby, *The Civil War*, Vol. 3, Random House, NY, 1986.

Goodwin, Donald W., *Adv. Intern. Med.*, 32 283 298, 1987, "Genetic Influences in Alcoholism."

Gordis, Enoch; Tabakoff, Boris, Goldman, David and Berg, Kate, *Journal of the American Medical Association*, April 18, 1990, Vol. 263, No. 15, pp 2094-2095, "An Editorial, Finding the Gene(s) for Alcoholism."

Jellinek, E.M. *The Disease Concept of Alcoholism*, Hillhouse Press, New Brunswick, 1960.

Johnson, Vernon, *I'll Quit Tomorow*, Harper & Row, NY, 1973.

Journal Graphics, Driving Drunk: License to Kill? ABC's "Turning Point, " Transcript # 141, Denver, 1994.

Kantrowitz, Barbara, *Newsweek*, November 28, 1994, "In Search of the Sacred."

Kinney, Jean and Leaton, Gwen. *Loosening the Grip*, C.V. Mosby, St. Louis, 1978.

Kopp, Sheldon B. *If You Meet the Buddha on the Road, Kill Him!* Science and Behavior Books, Ben Lomond, CA, 1972.

Kurtz, Ernest. *Not God: A History of Alcoholics Anonymous*, Hazelden, Center City, MN, 1979.

Lawson, Gary W, Ellis, Dan C. and Rivers, P. Clayton. *Essentials of Chemical Dependency Counseling*, Aspen, Rockville, MD, 1992.

Lawson, Gary and Lawson, Ann W. *Adolescent Substance Abuse: Etiology, Treatment and Prevention*, Aspen, Gaithersberg, MD, 1992.

Lawson, Gary, Peterson, James S. and Lawson, Ann. *Alcoholism and the Family*, Aspen, Rockville, MD, 1983.

Levin, Jerome D, *Treatment of Alcoholism and Other Addictions*, Northvale, 1991.

May, Rollo, *The Meaning of Anxiety*, Pocket Books, NY, 1950.

May, Rollo, *Paulus: Reminiscences of a Friendship*, Harper and Row, NY, 1973.

May, Rollo, *Power and Innocence*, W.W. Norton, NY, 1972.

May, Rollo, *The Courage to Create*, W.W. Norton, NY, 1975.

Menninger, Karl, *Man Against Himself*, Harvest Books, NY, 1938.

Menninger, Karl, *The Vital Balance*, Viking, NY, 1963.

Metzger, Lawrence. *From Denial to Recovery*, Jossey-Bass, San Francisco, 1988.

Noble, Ernest P, *Scientific American*, March/April 1996, "The Gene That Rewards Alcoholism," pp. 52-61.

Palfai, Tibor & Jankiewicz, Henry. *Drugs and Human Behavior*, W.C. Brown, Dubuque, 1991.

Powell, David J, *The Counselor*, July/August 1994, Volume 12, No. 4, "The Care and Feeding of the Counselor," Arlington, VA.

Powell, David J, *Clinical Supervision: Skills for Substance Abuse Counselors*, Human Sciences Press, NY, 1980.

Radcliffe, Anthony; Rush, Peter; Sites, Carol and Crusel, Joe, *The Pharmer's Almanac: A Training Manual on the Pharmacology of Psychoactive Drugs*, M.A.C. Publications, Denver, 1985.

Ray, Oakley and Ksir, Charles, *Drugs, Society and Human Behavior*, Times Mirror, St. Louis, 1987.

Rivers, P. Clayton, *Alcohol and Human Behavior*, Prentice Hall, Englewood Cliffs, NJ, 1994.

Sunshine, Linda and Wright, John W, *The 100 Best Treatment Centers for Alcoholism and Drug Abuse*, Avon, NY, 1988.

Tiebout, Harry M, *The Act of Surrender in the Therapeutic Process*, Originally an undated National Council on Alcoholism pamphlet, now available through Hazelden, Center City, MN.

Tillich, Paul, *The Courage To Be*, Yale University Press, New Haven, 1952.

Tillich, Paul, *The Dynamics of Faith*, Harper Torchbooks, NY, 1957.

Tillich, Paul, *The New Being*, Charles Scribners, NY, 1955.

Tillich, Paul, *The Shaking of the Foundations*, Charles Scribners, NY, 1948.

Vaillant, George E, "Dangers of Psychotherapy in the Treatment of Alcoholism" in *Dynamic Approaches to the Understanding and Treatment of Alcoholism*, M.H. Bean and N.E. Zinberg, editors. NY, MacMillan, 1981.

Vaillant, George E, *The Natural History of Alcoholism,* Harvard University Press, Cambridge, 1983.

Vaillant, George E, *The Natural History of Alcoholism Revisited,* Harvard University Press, Cambridge, 1995.

Ward, Geoffrey; Burns, Ric and Burns, Ken, *The Civil War,* Knopf, NY, 1991.

Wegscheider-Cruse, Sharon, *Another Chance: Hope and Health for the Alcoholic Family,* Science and Behavior Books, Palo Alto, CA, 1981.

About the Author

Robert M. Claytor, M.Ed., M.Div., is a Licensed Professional Counselor and a retired Fellow of the American Association of Pastoral Counselors. He is also certified by the International Certification Reciprocity Consortium as a clinical supervisor of substance abuse counselors. Mr. Claytor created the Substance Abuse Counselor Education Program at Mary Baldwin College. His primary interest is now in his writing. His hobby is amateur theater. The author has four children and five grandchildren and lives with his wife, Marilyn, in Staunton, Virginia. She directs the Chemical Dependency programs at Charter Hospital of Charlottesville.

Book layout, jacket photograph, jacket design by Bradley Robison